W9-BCB-700

Germany

SWEDEN
DENMARK
BALTIC SEA
NORTH FRISIAN IS.
Flensburg
RUGEN I.
NORTH SEA
Kiel
Lübeck
Rostock
EAST FRISIAN IS.
Bremerhaven
Hamburg
EAST GERMANY
Bremen
Weser R.
Elbe R.
Oder R.
Hannover
Berlin
POLAN
NETHERLANDS
WEST GERMANY
Magdeburg
Neisse R.
Essen
Dortmund
Halle
Leipzig
Ruhr R.
Görlitz
Rhine R.
Düsseldorf
Cologne
Erfurt
Dresden
BELGIUM
Aachen
Bonn
Fulda
Suhl
Wiesbaden
Frankfurt
Mosel R.
Mainz
Main R.
LUX.
Trier
Worms
Würzburg
CZECHOSLOVAKIA
Saarbrücken
Mannheim
Heidelberg
Nuremberg
Regensburg
Stuttgart
Baden
Ulm
Augsburg
Munich
Rhine R.
Freiburg
Danube R.
AUSTRIA
FRANCE
Oberammergau
Berchtesgaden
LAKE CONSTANCE
SWITZERLAND
ITALY
N
0
100 Miles

THE HORIZON CONCISE HISTORY OF

by Francis Russell

Published by
AMERICAN HERITAGE PUBLISHING CO., INC.
New York

Library of Congress Cataloging in Publication Data
Russell, Francis, 1910–
The Horizon concise history of Germany.
1. Germany—History. I. Horizon (New York, 1958–). II. Title.
DD90.R87 943 72-13914
ISBN 0-07-054307-0

CHAPTER I

THE TRIBAL HEARTLAND

Germany on the map looks today, as it has always looked, a heartland—to use that much abused geopolitical term. First it was a region, then an idea, and only belatedly a nation in the modern sense; within our time it has again become divided. About the year A.D. 96 Tacitus described Germania Magna as "separated from Gaul, Raetia [Switzerland], and Pannonia [Bohemia] by the rivers Rhine and Danube; from Sarmatia [Poland and European Russia] and Dacia [Hungary] by mutual suspicion." He found the climate severe and the scenery grim, rough forests for the most part, interspersed with foul swamps. "The Germans are an indigenous people," he wrote, "very little affected by admixture with other races through immigration or intercourse." Much admiring the sturdy simplicity of their tribal life, he described them as fair-haired, fiercely blue-eyed people who hated peace. Caesar had written earlier that "the whole life of the Germans is spent in hunting and the practice of war."

The Germans of Caesar and Tacitus are not the modern Germans, although Wagner and William II and Hitler liked to think so. That original mixture has become so diluted that it has lost most of its iden-

In "Saint Eustace" the masterful German artist Albrecht Dürer interprets the conversion of a Roman soldier upon seeing a miraculous stag in the forest.

tity. Germany is perhaps the most racially mixed country in Europe. Its four components are the residual pre-Indo-European population, the Celts, the Germanic tribes, and the Slavs. It has absorbed and reflects the cultural pattern of the Celt, the Slav, and the Roman. The west and southwest with their Roman-founded cities like Cologne and Trier are Latin and Celtic in character; central and southern Germany are more Celtic than Latin, although this blends with the Slavic in the southeast, while the east has produced the Slavic-Germanic mixture so characteristic of Prussia.

However tenuous the link between present-day Germans and the blue-eyed tribesmen of Tacitus, German history begins in the forests between the Rhine and the Vistula. From this tribal heartland, Goths and Vandals moved south into the Mediterranean countries, the Burgundians into the Rhone region, the Franks into Gaul, and finally the Saxons invaded England. According to Tacitus the first tribesmen to cross the Rhine and drive out the Celts of Gaul were the Tungri, who then called themselves Germani.

Julius Caesar by his Gallic conquests had pushed the frontiers of Rome to the Rhine, making possible the establishment of the *limes,* the fortified Roman boundary against the barbarians extending from the Rhine as far as the Danube, which it touched at Regensburg. The western and southwestern lands that fell within its limits became parts of the Roman Empire, and many of the tribesmen became Roman soldiers and even Roman citizens. Augustus added Raetia and Pannonia to the empire, then dispatched his general, Publius Quintilius Varus, to Germany with three legions to extend the Roman boundaries and tribute to the Elbe. The chief of the Cherusci, Arminius—known in German legend as Hermann—who had served as an officer in the Roman auxiliary, persuaded many of the recently subjected tribes to unite with him in opposing the Roman advance. In A.D. 9 in the Teutoberg Forest he ambushed and annihilated three legions, some twenty thousand men, or roughly a tenth of the whole Roman army. Though Augustus raised new legions to fortify the frontier, he made no further attempt to extend Roman rule beyond the *limes.*

The tribes of Germany combined into five major groups: the Frisians along the Baltic; the Alemans, of Suevian stock, on the Upper Rhine; the Franks, whose very name signified "free of the Romans"; the Saxons, between the Weser and the Elbe; and the Thuringians, south of the Saxons. From the kindred tribal dialects two major speech forms developed: High German in the south, destined to become over the centuries the standard literary speech; and in the north Low German, a speech that remained a dialect but that is much closer to the Anglo-Saxon than High German. *Deutsch,* the German-chosen word for things German, originally meant popular speech as opposed to Latin.

For over four hundred years the Romans remained on the west bank of the Rhine facing Germany. In the border areas Roman rule grew to be accepted as part of the order of things. From Augst (Augusta Rauricorum) a few miles above Basel (Basilea) to Cologne (Colonia Agrippinensis), named in honor of Nero's mother, Roman garrisons developed into cities. Oberwesel was first the military station Vosolvia, Bacharach with its vineyards evolved from Ara Bacchi (Altar of Bacchus), Strasbourg as Argentoratum became a legion headquarters, while Coblenz—Ad Confluentes—guarded the junction of the Rhine and the Moselle. Trier (Augusta Treverorum) on the Moselle, founded by Augustus on a tribal site, would become an imperial city, the northern headquarters for a succession of emperors, after Diocletian's division of the empire in A.D. 269. Within their fortified cities the Romans built palaces, baths, and amphitheaters, and in the more open country luxurious villas. Since it was easier to divide the Germans than to conquer them, it became Roman policy to foment quarrels among the tribes and to flatter the more powerful chiefs.

German life within the forest region east of the Rhine remained almost unchanged during the Roman centuries. Tribes combined, fought each other, combined again, penetrated the fortified frontiers in brief and terrible raids. They created no cities of their own.

However primitive their lives, the Germans had needs which the sophisticated Roman traders were ready to supply. German women demanded cooking and eating utensils, while their warrior husbands came to prefer Italian wine to native-brewed beer. In exchange for the goods they wanted, the Germans offered Baltic amber, women's hair, and slaves. Ever since Arminius' great victory they had known that the Roman legions were not unconquerable. Now with growing trade they became increasingly conscious of the empire and its great cities, the provinces, and those enticing warmer regions of olive and citron that would from then on fascinate the German mind. They also realized how vulnerable the border garrisons were to sudden attack.

The tribes of Germany in their multiplicity remained a restless mass, probing always for weak spots in the *limes*. Their road to expansion ran south and west, until it came up against the Roman frontier. Again and again that barrier was breached. In 167 a host of Germanic tribes, spearheaded by the Quadi and the Marcomanni, crossed the Danube to ravage and plunder Raetia, Pannonia, Dacia, and Noricum, overwhelming a Roman army sent to check them. Only when the emperor Marcus Aurelius took to the field in person were the legions able to push the barbarians back across the Danube.

Meanwhile the Alemans, a formidable enemy with a new name that meant "all men," had arisen in the Upper Rhine region. They were not a single tribe but rather a confederacy. On their first appearance in history they invaded Raetia but were repelled in 213 by the emperor Caracalla. Twenty years later they renewed their attack on the Roman defenses with such force that Emperor Alexander Severus broke off his campaign against the Persians to deal with them. After his assassination, his successor, the rough campaigner Maximinus, advanced by forced marches to the country of the Alemans, destroyed their fields and houses, and finally defeated them deep in their own territory. This year of victory, 238, marked the last great Roman campaign to defend the Rhine-Danube frontier. Its salutary effect lasted twenty years. Then the Alemans gathered their strength and smashed through the Roman fortifications along the Danube, overwhelming the Roman garrisons, sweeping irresistibly over the southern region, even sending across the Alps into Italy a force that was finally defeated near Milan by the armies of Emperor Gallienus. The region just north of the Alps, however, continued in the Alemans' possession as did the passes to Italy.

While the Alemans were spreading south, the Franks appeared on the Lower Rhine. Their name would soon sound more ominous to Roman ears than that of the Alemans. *Franci* they were, "free men," a league of nations composed of the tribes and smaller clans of these regions. The first Frankish attack on the Rhine frontier came in 253, and soon the whole west bank was in their hands. Vast bands of Franks crossed the river unimpeded into Gaul, devastating the regions from the Rhine to the Pyrenees and even pushing their destructive course into Spain. All Europe then stood in terror of the Germans. Eventually the Roman legions mustered enough strength to force the Franks back. Again the Rhine was the dividing line. But it was an uneasy boundary increasingly breached as the rickety empire continued its decline.

Meanwhile, far east of Germany itself in the region of the Black Sea, another Germanic people, the Goths, was preparing to make its indelible mark on history. Originating in Scandinavia the Goths had migrated to the Baltic coast, then from the Gulf of Danzig had moved up the Vistula to the neighborhood of the Marcomanni. At some vague later date they moved on to the whole northern coast of the Black Sea, drawing other Germanic peoples to them even as they themselves divided east and west into the Ostrogoths and Visigoths.

A bloody haze seems to hang over Europe in the next two centuries. Tribes move across the landscape with seemingly aimless compulsion. Emperors and coemperors are cast up and cast down to the rattle of spears by their Praetorian Guard. Out of the haze certain events loom up like signal towers: the emergence of Christianity as the state religion in the fourth century under the emperor Constantine, and his temporary reunification of the Eastern and Western Empires; the sack of Rome itself by the Visigoths and again by the Vandals; the thrust of the Asiatic Huns at the gates of Europe, threatening the whole West.

Early in his reign, Constantine moved relentlessly to suppress the restive Franks, capturing two of their chiefs and throwing them to the beasts in the arena. He was equally firm with the Alemans and their allies, while at the same time he strengthened the whole belt of fortresses along the frontier. The *limes* remained quiet; but with his death in 337 and the years of civil war that followed, the tribes again overran the left bank of the Rhine, capturing Cologne and penetrating far into the interior of Gaul, plundering until there was nothing left to plunder. Finally the young caesar Julian—since Diocletian, the emperor's successor-designate had come to be called caesar—took command in Gaul, drove back the Franks, defeated seven Frankish "kings," recaptured Cologne and Strasbourg, and was on the way to pacifying the whole Rhine country until in 361 civil conflict forced him to return to Rome. Again the Franks and Alemans made forays across the Rhine and again the Roman legions drove them back. The Western emperor Valentinian, who ruled from 364 to 375, restored the Rhine frontiers and further strengthened and improved the defenses. Under his son and successor, Gratian, the Rhine region remained relatively peaceful. The peace was briefly broken in 378 when the Alemans crossed the Rhine in force. Gratian overwhelmed them near Colmar in Alsace.

As the Huns moved westward, terror swept the Gothic nations. The Ostrogoths rallied and tried to hold back the implacable Asiatics at spear point, but the Huns were not to be denied. They subdued the Ostrogoths, and the Visigoths in panic begged to be allowed to enter the empire; Valens gave them permission. In improvised boats they swarmed across the Danube to the plains of Thrace "like the rain of ashes from an eruption of Etna." Unfortunately, the lesser Roman officials showed none of Valens' magnanimity but harried and abused the tribesmen until inevitably the Visigoths, who through Roman negligence had not been disarmed, revolted. Even the Gothic auxiliaries joined the rebellion. Valens led his forces in person against the insurgents, but after a few initial successes the Romans were overwhelmed in 378 at Adrianople, two thirds of their army being destroyed and Valens himself killed. The Battle of Adrianople shook the empire to its foundations. Even though the Goths did not follow up their victory, it was now obvious that the five centuries of struggle between Roman and German were drawing to a close.

At the beginning of the fifth century German tribes in increasing numbers began to surge forward against the provinces of the Western Empire. Sometimes, as Gratian had done with the Ostrogoths and Huns invading Pannonia, the emperor was able to make uneasy federates of his enemies by yielding land and tributes. In 401 the Vandals, who had thrust into Raetia, were granted much of the region on condition that they serve in the Roman army. Four years later Ostrogoths and Vandals with related tribes pushed across the Alps, and Italy was saved only by the skill of two tribal generals in the Roman service, one a Goth and the other a Hun. The following year the Vandals devastated Gaul, forcing the Frankish tribes aside, and finding no other armies to oppose them continued on into the Iberian Peninsula. Burgundians drove out the Alemans along the lower Main River, and the Alemans in turn invaded and conquered Roman upper Germany.

Under Theodoric I, the Visigoths had established the kingdom of Toulouse, a Gothic state within the Roman Empire, in which the Goths

Germanic tribes had as their protector the warrior god Woden, shown on horseback in this eighth-century carved burial stone.

were granted two thirds of the land. In eastern Gaul the Burgundians became Roman federates, as had the Ostrogoths in Pannonia. The pattern repeated itself throughout the waning empire.

Most of the German tribes had felt compelled to submit to the Hun king Attila even as both the Western and Eastern Empires had felt compelled to pay him tribute. By their submission and by serving in the Hun army, the Germans had at least been able to preserve their autonomy. It was the Visigoths who at last succeeded in shattering the myth of Hun invincibility, after Attila with a vast army had invaded Gaul in 451. Confronting him at Troyes, the Visigoths under King Theodoric fought the Hun army to a standstill. The following year a more circumspect Attila took the easier course of invading Italy, but before he reached Rome his army was swept by the plague, and when an embassy of Romans led by Pope Leo I arrived at his camp he used this as an excuse to retire. With his death the following year, the threatening Hunnish empire dissolved.

Even if the Huns had not impelled the German tribes westward, the growing pressure of the German forest folk would have inevitably engulfed the *limes.* For as the German population increased, the Roman and Celtic survivors had been declining, while land within the empire fell out of cultivation. It was a vacuum the Germans were bound to fill. Across the ancient barrier they came, establishing kingdoms that still kept a minimal allegiance to imperial Rome while at the same time bringing their kings, their laws, their customs, and their often Arian Christianity with them. German tribes settled beyond Gaul in Spain and Africa. Germans filled the ranks of the legions and rose to the highest offices, even that of supreme commander. And in the process the Germans beyond the Rhine gradually became Romanized.

Tacitus in his account of Germany enumerated over forty tribes. Four centuries later even their names had vanished, replaced by the more familiar designations of tribal aggregates, the Franks, the Saxons, and the Alemans. The Visigoths from their capital at Toulouse had expanded southward over most of the Iberian Peninsula. East of the Rhone lay the Burgundian kingdom, with the neighboring Alemans settled in what would later be Alsace. The Franks occupied the Lower Rhine to the North Sea, themselves divided into the Ripuarian, or riverbank, and Salian, or seacoast, Franks. North of them were the

Saxons. The Vandals had crossed the Mediterranean to North Africa. After the day in 476 when Odoacer deposed the stripling emperor Romulus Augustulus, the Roman Empire of the West came to an end, and the Ostrogoths ruled Italy. Other more vaguely defined tribes of free Germans clung to their ancestral life in the forests of central Europe, impervious to history.

In the new Germanic states kingship became the accepted, in fact, the only practical, form of government as kings developed from the chiefs of the coalescing tribes. Yet the new kingdoms by necessity followed the Roman administrative customs and procedures. The imperial structure continued under Odoacer and would persist through the centuries as a haunting presence until renewed by Charlemagne. Under the new rulers most of the Roman civil service remained intact. The old Roman provincial aristocracy, shorn of much of their land, furnished high officials for the Germanic kings as well as bishops for the Church, though Germans controlled the armies. Roman literary figures took their places in Germanic courts. Marriage, however, between the barbarians and the Romans was forbidden.

That these Germanic kingdoms, made up of tribes so often given to fratricidal wars in the past, would live without conflict was impossible. Inevitably one tribe would come to dominate the rest, would reconstitute the shadowy memory of the empire. In the middle of the sixth century the emperor of the East, Justinian I, annihilated two of the contenders—the kingdoms of the Vandals and the Ostrogoths—and the destiny of domination fell to the Franks.

The history of the Franks is the prehistory of the modern German people. With their empire they laid the foundations of both France and Germany, and in this the leading role was taken by the Salian Franks. From the shores of the North Sea the Salian Franks moved gradually south, sometimes clashing with the Romans but still remaining federates. Then at about the beginning of the fifth century they refused any longer to recognize Rome's authority, and repudiated both the Latin tongue and the Christian religion. For all their fierce love of combat, they were still held in check by the great fortified Roman road that ran from Arras and Cambrai to Cologne. One of their chiefs, Clodion, after an initial defeat by the Romans, rallied and led his army against Cambrai, capturing the town and gaining control of the

Roman road. The Franks could now march south as far as the Somme.

Clodion was succeeded by his son Merovaeus, the founder of the Merovingian dynasty, who sought the support and protection of the Roman Empire and sent a contingent of Franks to oppose the invasion by Attila. Merovaeus' son Childeric fought beside Roman generals in the valley of the Loire against the Visigoths and devoted himself as a loyal federate to policing Gaul in Rome's behalf.

Childeric's son Clovis was only fifteen when he became one of the Salian chiefs. For five years he watched and waited, then led the other Frankish kings in attacking the cluster of Gallo-Roman cities between the Somme and the Loire ruled by the Roman official Syagrius. Clovis occupied Soissons, extended his rule through Belgium, and overcame the cities along his route until he finally reached Paris. A singularly farseeing young man, he was conciliatory in his conquests, leaving the Gallo-Romans in possession of their land and, although himself a pagan, showing the greatest respect for the Christian religion. He married a Christian princess from Burgundy, Clotilda, who did her best to convert him. Finally on Christmas Day, 496, he was baptized into the Catholic Church and commanded his people to follow him. Whatever the depth of his belief, the practical advantages of such a step had long been apparent to him in the support he would derive from the powerful bishops in his struggle against the heathen tribes and the Visigoths, who, though Christians, had easily adopted the Arian heresy denying the divinity of Christ. Such support had been welcome when he raised an army to attack the Alemans. In a completely successful campaign he drove them out of Alsace and to the high valleys of the Alps.

Clovis was determined to make Gaul a single state of which he would be the ruler. Although he failed to subject Burgundy, he next turned his attentions to the Visigoths, routing them completely near Poitiers and cutting down the king, Alaric II, with his own hand. After the battle he again treated the conquered territory with clemency, seizing no land but merely requiring the Arians to submit to the orthodox faith. He established the seat of his government in Paris, and as a measure of caution had his rival Salian chiefs assassinated while at the same time asserting his sovereignty over the dynastically troubled Ripuarian Franks. At his death Clovis had conquered nearly all of Gaul except Burgundy and Provence. By driving out the Alemans he had

Although German law prevailed among the barbarians, some subjects lived by Roman law, codified for them by the Visigoth Alaric II in this manuscript.

LODH
ANRI
REX DUX
ALAMAN
NORUM
EPI QUI
FUERUNT
EI CON
GREGATI
NUR
XXXIII
COMITES
UERO
LXXII
DUCES
FUERUNT
XXXIII
CONGRE
GATI
CETERE
UULGO
MULTI
TUDO
MAGNA
HOS LEGE
GE TU
LECTOR

extended his authority beyond the Rhine, and in codifying the Salic law, he had confirmed that authority. Yet the shadow of the empire haunted him too, and after the emperor of the East had made him an honorary consul, he assumed the symbolic purple mantle and tunic.

Clovis had regarded the Frankish kingdom as a family inheritance, and left it divided equally among his four sons. They carried on their father's work of conquering Gaul by subjugating the Burgundians and annexing Provence, but they also intrigued against one another. Death in the end settled their contentions by leaving one son, Lothair, in sole possession of Clovis' kingdom. Lothair in turn divided his Frankish inheritance among his four sons in four capital cities: Metz, Orléans, Paris, and Soissons. The king of Paris soon died, and Gaul once more, as in Caesar's day, was divided into three parts, this time into the Gallo-Roman Neustria in the west, the Germanic Austrasia in the east, and Burgundy with its capital at Orléans.

The early seventh century reunification of the Frankish kingdom under Lothair's grandson, Lothair II, the succession of his powerful and determined son Dagobert, and after Dagobert's death the decline of the Merovingian dynasty into the juvenile *Rois Fainéants,* the Do-Nothing Kings, concern German history only as they prepare the way for the succeeding house of Pepin and the towering figure of Charlemagne. The period itself was one of decay and decline, a dark age.

In the time of the weak and enervated Merovingian child-kings, authority devolved on the chief officer of the household, the mayor of the palace. Under their individual palace mayors, the separateness of Neustria, Austrasia, and Burgundy became more and more evident, as royal authority eroded and the independence of the nobility increased. Most notable were the mayors of Austrasia, who soon made that office hereditary. The founder of this mayoral dynasty was Pepin, mayor of the palace when the young Dagobert was merely king of Austrasia. When Pepin's son Grimoald as mayor prematurely attempted to seize the throne, he was thwarted by the Austrasian nobles and executed. But a quarter of a century later in 687, Pepin II, grandson of Pepin, emerged with almost absolute power in Austrasia and took the field against the rival mayor of Neustria, defeating him at Tertry near Orléans, a battle that marks the real end of the Merovingians.

The second Pepin had once more united the kingdom. During his lifetime he appointed his grandsons mayors in Neustria and Austrasia, but after his death they were not strong enough to resist the spreading anarchy, and it fell to Pepin's illegitimate son Charles to restore order. Charles ruled forcefully in the manner of his father, leading an army against the recalcitrant Neustrians, making himself master of Burgundy, appointing his own counts and bishops, and for some years governing without a king. When the Moors invaded Gaul from Spain, which they had conquered in 711, Charles defeated them. In the great battle which took place in 732, near Tours, their leader was slain and their advance broken. Following this victory, he became known as Charles Martel, Charles the Hammer. He forced the Saxons to pay tribute, abolished the troublesome duchy of Alemannia, and granted safe-conducts to Boniface and other Anglo-Saxon missionaries intent on converting the pagan Germans in Thuringia and beyond.

Though still without the royal title, Charles exercised the custom of the Frankish kings before him: he divided his lands between his sons Carloman and Pepin; Austrasia, Alemannia, Thuringia, and the suzerainty of Bavaria going to the former; Neustria, Burgundy, Provence, and the suzerainty of Aquitaine to the latter.

After six years of joint rule, Carloman abdicated to become a monk, and Pepin III became the sole mayor of the palace. Eager now to be actual king as well as ruler, he sent an embassy to Rome to ask Pope Zacharias if he had the right to assume the kingship. The pope replied that since he was king in fact it would be well for him to be king in name. To confirm this among the laity, Pepin fell back on the tribal tradition of calling an assembly of the Franks. This assembly unanimously chose him king. The last, feeble Merovingian was then shut up in a monastery, and Pepin, chosen by his people, and "by the grace of God," was anointed and crowned by Archbishop Boniface.

Shortly before his death Pepin divided his kingdom between his sons, Charles and Carloman. The two kings were enthroned and anointed in 768 a month after their father's death. Three years later Carloman died, a fugitive figure who left no mark on history. His brother, on the other hand, would influence the historical development of Europe. As Charlemagne, as Carolus Magnus, as Karl der Grosse, the resurrector of the Roman Empire of the West, he became a father-figure, the legendary hero of both France and Germany.

APOLO

CHAPTER II

CHARLEMAGNE, THE VISIONARY

Charlemagne was born in 742. The day and the place are unrecorded. His mother Bertrada, Pepin's chief mistress and later his wife, became the first Carolingian queen of Frankland. Of the childhood and youth of her first-born, Charles, nothing is known. Einhard, Charlemagne's earnest dwarfish secretary for almost a quarter of a century and later his chronicler, considered that it would be "folly to write a word concerning Charles' birth and infancy, or even his boyhood, for nothing has ever been written on the subject, and there is no one alive now who can give information of it."

The boy Charles makes his first appearance in history at the age of twelve when he and his brother are sent by his father, "the most Christian king of the Franks," to Valais in the Swiss Alps to meet the aged Pope Stephen II and conduct him to their father's palace. Stephen, long harassed by the Lombards, the Germanic conquerors of northern Italy, had been held practically a prisoner in Pavia by their king, Aistulf, before finally being allowed to proceed northward across the Alps to Frankland. At the Valais Abbey the ailing and travel-weary pontiff was greeted by a smiling, fair-haired boy, tall and of pleasant

Charlemagne, physically impressive, intellectually curious, politically shrewd, became for history the ideal ruler, a German Apollo (here rendered by Dürer).

manner, who introduced himself as King Pepin's elder son, Charles.

The entourage then continued on to the court of Pepin, whom Stephen sought to engage in an anti-Lombard alliance. To protect the patrimony of Saint Peter against the Lombards seemed to Pepin as pious an act as fighting the infidels, and he made preparation for an Italian campaign that would restore Stephen to the papal inheritance. Stephen in turn granted him the title of Roman patrician, and by re-annointing him in the abbey church of Saint Denis in Paris and by crowning his two sons as their father's heirs, sanctified the house of Pepin and Arnulf as the royal house of the Franks.

There is no mention of young Charles traveling with the Frankish army that set out for Italy in the spring of 755, but it is unlikely that King Pepin would have left the boy at home. Pepin had learned the art of war from his own father, Charles Martel, and once in Italy he outmaneuvered the Lombards at every turn, finally laying siege to Pavia and forcing Aistulf to seek a truce. Pepin's terms, those he had previously determined with the pope, were harsh, and no sooner had he left Italy then Aistulf renounced his pledge. Pepin again marched on Italy and this time thoroughly routed the Lombards. As he lay encamped before Pavia, he was visited by emissaries of the Eastern emperor, Constantine V, who demanded that Ravenna, which Pepin had given to Pope Stephen as part of the patrimony of Saint Peter, be restored to Byzantium in whose possession it had been before the Lombard conquest. Pepin, well knowing that his Donation was illegal, replied that he had fought for Saint Peter and for the pardon of his sins, and that nothing "would induce him to take away what he had once given to Saint Peter." Constantine was forced to accept the reply —he could do little else—but the widening gap between East and West grew even more apparent.

Charles was twenty-six and Carloman barely sixteen when the king their father died. Pepin left no will, but according to ancient Frankish tradition, confirmed by tribal assembly, Frankland was henceforth divided; Austrasia with part of Neustria and the north German lands going to Charles, while Carloman received western Neustria, Provence, and the Swabian country of the Alemans. Carloman died within three years. He was rumored to have been plotting against his brother, and at his death his widow with her two infant sons fled to Italy. Charles concerned himself no further about them. Another national assembly of the Franks unanimously confirmed him as sovereign of his again united country.

Charlemagne was thirty years old when he became the ruler of all Frankland. Teutonic to the core, with his native German dialect as his first language, he also spoke Latin and the Romance dialect that was evolving in Neustria from Latin and Celtic, and he could at least understand if not converse with the Greek-speaking emissaries of Byzantium. A man of great physical strength, a valiant swimmer, alert and gray-eyed, with a grave demeanor but a short temper, he was marked by two traits: a boundless energy and an indomitable curiosity. According to Einhard he detested idleness above all else. In appearance he was: "large and strong, and of lofty stature, though not disproportionately tall (his height is well known to have been seven times the length of his foot); the upper part of his head was round, his eyes very large and animated, nose a little too long, hair fair, and face laughing and merry. Thus his appearance was always stately and dignified, whether he was standing or sitting; although his neck was thick and somewhat short, and his belly rather prominent; but the symmetry of the rest of his body concealed these defects. His gait was firm, his whole carriage manly, and his voice clear, but not so strong as his size led one to expect."

His appetite was large, but unlike most men of his day he was abstemious with wine. Further, according to his secretary-chronicler, "Charles had the gift of ready and fluent speech and could express whatever he had to say with the utmost clearness. He was not satisfied with command of his native language merely but gave attention to the study of foreign ones, and in particular was such a master of Latin that he could speak it as well as his native tongue. . . . He was so eloquent indeed that he might have passed for a teacher of eloquence. He most zealously cultivated the liberal arts, held those who taught them in great esteem, and conferred great honors upon them. He took lessons in grammar from Deacon Peter of Pisa, at that time an aged man. Another deacon, Albin of Britain, surnamed Alcuin, a man of Saxon extraction, who was the greatest scholar of the day, was his teacher in other branches of learning. The King spent much time and labor with him studying rhetoric, dialectics, and especially astronomy; he learned to reckon, and used to investigate the motions of the heavenly bodies most curiously, with an intelligent scrutiny. He also tried to write, and used to keep tablets and blanks in bed under his pillow, that at leisure hours he might accustom his hand to form the letters; however, as he did not begin his efforts in due season, but late in life, they met with ill success."

At Charlemagne's accession, Frankland consisted of what are today France (except Brittany) and the Low Countries as well as a considerable section of Germany across the Rhine. In forty-three years of rule he doubled the size of the empire, through his wars absorbing the Saxon lands, Bohemia, the great Danubian plain that the Romans called Pannonia, Lombardy and the northern Italian peninsula, and the Spanish March across the Pyrenees. Yet, though he became the most powerful ruler in the world, the successor to the Roman emperors, he was not a world conqueror like Caesar or Alexander. It would never have occurred to him to weep because he had no more worlds to conquer. Whatever the flaws in his character, he was dominated by a nobler impulse. He dreamt of a Europe after the pattern of his favorite

Ninth-century warfare as depicted in the Saint Gall Psalter: below, a walled city is besieged; opposite, victors and vanquished negotiate among the dead.

book, Saint Augustine's *The City of God,* a Europe made one in faith as well as territory, a greater Frankland where the swords would have at last been beaten into plowshares and all people would walk in the peaceable kingdom in the name of the Lord. He saw his campaigns not as acts of conquest but in the nature of crusades. Bishops, priests, and monks accompanied his army, and he thanked God devoutly for his victories. Never did he try to impose Frankish social patterns on those he conquered. Diversity within the single state was his goal. His was the first great vision of a united Europe.

For all his questioning mind, the one thing Charlemagne never questioned was his Christian faith. This remained the cornerstone of all his beliefs, and no shadows of doubt ever troubled him. Theory and practice, as in any belief, were not always consistent. Like Caesar and Alexander before him, Charlemagne was a man of strong physical passions and saw no need to curb them. A woman was for him a necessity like food, and like food to be accepted casually. He had four or five wives, a number of mistresses, and any number of cubicular encounters. He refused to allow his numerous daughters to enter into marriage, but was

indifferent to the frequency and variety of their lovers. At times he was capable of acts of pagan cruelty. Probably he regretted them afterward. God, he was convinced, would understand the weaknesses of such sturdy flesh as his.

Carloman was still alive when Charlemagne undertook to finish their father's efforts to control Aquitaine, the rebellious duchy in southwestern France which had posed a constant threat to the unity of Frankland. Although Carloman refused his brother's request for aid, Charlemagne quickly and permanently conquered the province and forced the duke of Aquitaine to flee to Gascony and to his death.

Pepin's Italian campaigns, for all their successes, had left the Lombards under their king Desiderius intact and truculent. Pope Stephen II's successor alternated between denouncing the Lombards and trying to form an alliance with them. Charlemagne's mother had gone to Italy, and in an effort to reconcile the two houses had brought back Desiderius' daughter as a bride for her son. Charlemagne's first wife had born him a cripple, and he was weary of her as well, but this second dynastic marriage lasted less than a year. Pope Stephen III denounced it, not so much on moral grounds as from fear of Frank-Lombard alliance. When in January, 772, Adrian I was elected pope, there were no more papal efforts to conciliate the Lombards. Adrian, a pure Roman, would remain Charlemagne's trusted friend for the next twenty-three years. Threatened at the beginning of his reign by Desiderius, Adrian appealed to the Franks, and Charlemagne—though involved in his perennial struggle with the Saxons—mustered an army and crossed the Alps to make war on the Lombards. The results of this war were, in Einhard's words, "the subjection of Italy, the banishment of King Desiderius for life, the expulsion of his son Adalgis from Italy, and the restoration of the conquests of the Lombard kings to Adrian." Theoretically Adrian controlled the Frankish church, "the eldest daughter of the Mother Church," but in every practical sense control remained in Charlemagne's hands. Though he carefully notified the pope of his decisions, it was he who appointed the bishops, instituted church reforms, and presided over Frankish synods. Whatever his private morals, he insisted on high standards among his clerics and did much to purge the Church of the pagan vestiges that persisted beneath the at-times thin surface of its Christianity.

On his return from Italy Charlemagne resumed his campaign against the Saxons of northern Germany, his most troublesome and persistent adversaries. "A fierce people," Einhard called them, "given to the worship of devils and hostile to our religion, who think nothing of breaking the laws of God and man." Proudly pagan, the Saxons preserved their most sacred object, a carved wooden column they called Irminsul, in the middle of one of their remote forests. Irminsul, a replica of the Norse ash tree, Yggdrasill, whose roots bound together heaven and hell and the nether world, they worshiped as the dwelling place of their god. Before his Lombard campaign, Charlemagne had led an expedition into the Saxon forest and cut down and burned Irminsul, then offered the Saxons a truce. Waiting until he was in Italy, the Saxons replied by invading Hesse and sacking Saint Boniface's abbey at Fritzlar, murdering the abbot and his monks. Charlemagne when he heard the news resolved to fight "that perfidious nation . . . and . . . to persevere until they were either made subject to the Christian religion, or were swept off the face of the earth."

For thirty-three years, off and on, Charlemagne was at war with the Saxons, leading eighteen expeditions against them, although only twice engaging in large-scale pitched battles. In 785, after many casualties and reverses, the Saxon chiefs sent messengers of capitulation saying that they agreed to submit to Christianity. Taking them at their pledged word, Charlemagne attended a mass of thanksgiving at Christmas, rejoicing that the Saxon troubles were at last settled.

However, his joy was premature, for the leading Saxon chief, Widukind, with vast lands in Westphalia, was reconciled neither to Christianity nor to Charlemagne. He formed an alliance with Göttrik, "the greatly dreaded King of Denmark," and eight years of conflict with the Franks followed. While Charlemagne was campaigning in a distant corner of his kingdom, Widukind launched an assault on the Rhineland, burning towns and cities, leveling churches and cloisters, and putting priests, monks, and nuns to the sword. Charlemagne in his anger issued a capitulary decreeing death for even the slightest offense against the Church or canon law. In essence the king demanded unconditional surrender from the Saxons, and the result was, as always, to summon up the resistance of despair. Even those Saxon chiefs who had capitulated were now willing to march with Widukind. In 782 near

Münden, the Saxons fell on a Frankish army and annihilated it, killing several of the most skilled commanders.

Charlemagne's revenge would become the blackest spot on his basically enlightened career, a grim lapse into primitive tribalism. Once more he led an army against the Saxons, and this time Widukind fled to Denmark. As an example and a warning Charlemagne, encamped at Verdun (near Bremen), called an assembly of the Franks and then had more than four thousand Saxon hostages beheaded on the spot. It was the most ruthless act of this "most Christian" king. Possibly it so appeared later to Charlemagne, for when Widukind was finally forced to surrender and, as a condition of his surrender, accept Christianity, Charlemagne treated him with great magnanimity. Not only did he allow the Saxon to keep his vast territories, but he even acted as his sponsor in baptism. For all its forced aspect, Widukind's conversion was apparently a sincere one. Never did he waver in his new faith nor in his acceptance of Charlemagne's overlordship.

On his campaigns, Charlemagne dressed like his men, shared their food, knelt with them in prayer, and celebrated their triumphs. Yet he was a military strategist rather than a great captain who loved war for its own elemental sake. War was not for him an end, but only a means to what he hoped would be God's peace. He grew old in his campaigns against the Saxons. Between those Saxon interludes he twice led an army against the Avars, a savage Mongolian tribe that had settled in the Hungarian plain and from there was threatening Bavaria. He also led an army to Spain when the legates of a rival caliph asked for help in their struggle against the caliph of Córdoba. After crossing the Pyrenees, Charlemagne laid siege to and conquered Pamplona, then quickly returned to Frankland for reasons that can only be surmised since they remain unrecorded. It was on this return that his rear guard with the baggage train was overwhelmed by the Basques in the rocky defile of Roncesvalles. Among those killed was one Hruodland, governor of Brittany March, whose death would immortalize that insignificant disaster in the legend of *The Song of Roland*. Charlemagne's last campaign was against the Vikings, the pirate raiders of the coasts of Gaul and Germany whose king Göttrik claimed Saxony and Frisia as his provinces and boasted that he would yet invade Frankland as far as Aachen. Göttrik's murder by one of his bodyguards ended that particular threat, but Charlemagne was disquietingly aware of the future peril to Frankland in those beaked northern ships.

Summing up the reign, Einhard recorded that Charlemagne had more than doubled his patrimony, making tributary "Aquitaine, Gascony, and the whole region of the Pyrenees as far as the River Ebro . . . , all Italy from Aosta to Lower Calabria . . . ; then Saxony, which . . . is reckoned to be twice as wide as the country inhabited by the Franks; in addition both Pannonias, Dacia beyond the Danube, and Istria, Liburnia, and Dalmatia, except the cities on the coast, which he left to the Greek emperor for friendship's sake. . . . In fine, he vanquished and made tributary all the wild and barbarous tribes dwelling in Germany between the Rhine and the Vistula, the ocean and the Danube, all of which speak very much the same language but differ widely in customs and dress."

Einhard noted his friendship with King Alfonso of Asturias (Spain) and with the kings of the Scots. His most singular and one of his most durable friendships was with the legendary Baghdad caliph, Harun al-Rashid, a ruler he never met but with whom he constantly corresponded. The caliph sent him magnificent gifts of perfumes, silk stuffs, and jewelry, and once even an elephant that managed to live for a number of years in the unlikely northern climate.

As king of Frankland, Charlemagne traveled continuously over his domain, and although he had a scattering of palaces it was not until

Charlemagne's long-time correspondent, the powerful ruler of Islam, Harun al-Rashid, sent the Frankish king a succession of gifts, including a live elephant and this chess piece.

794—the latter part of his life—that he finally settled down in his great palace at Aachen. The site had long been a favorite of his, for its landscape, its boar-hunting, and not the least for its warm sulphur springs. When he determined to build his palace and basilica, Pope Adrian sent him marble from the palace of Ravenna along with the mosaics found there both on the pavements and on the walls of the church. Charlemagne's great hall and his basilica became the wonders of the West. The hall with its marble flooring and walls ornamented with bronze and gold was used for dining, for business matters and matters of state, and for entertainment and formal audiences. The basilica glowed with the magnificence of tessellated marble flooring, elaborately carved chair stalls, mosaics, great gold and silver candelabra studded with precious stones, and doors of solid brass. Its dome was topped by a huge golden ball, as if to mark the center of the thriving town that sprang up around it.

For all the magnificence of his Aachen residence, Charlemagne himself lived simply. He despised the elaborateness of the Byzantine ritual with its formalized servility, and refused to allow any man to bend the knee to him, declaring that homage was due to God alone. Usually he wore rough Frankish clothes though he could on the most formal occasions appear as a king of kings, crowned and dressed in cloth of gold, and seated on a golden throne under a crimson canopy. Perhaps closest to his heart was the palace school he founded in Aachen to preserve the ancient learning he loved and to educate the future proconsuls and administrators of his Frankish state. Boys were educated at the school without cost and were fed, clothed, and lodged at the king's expense. Merit rather than birth determined the selection of candidates. Charlemagne spared no expense in what concerned his school, regardless of the often perilous state of the exchequer. Ancient manuscripts were copied in large quantities in the clear script that would become known as Carolingian minuscule and that, though not invented in the palace school, was established as standard there. True to his idea of a united Europe, the king imported the best scholars he could find—and he found the best—from Ireland, Spain, England, and Italy. The Northumbrian scholar Alcuin of York became the school's first head. Among the other scholars who graced it were the Irishmen Clement the historian, Dungal the astronomer, and Dicuil the geographer; the

Spanish poet Theodulf; the monk of Monte Cassino known as Paul the Deacon; Einhard himself; Paulinus of Aquileia; the elderly grammarian Peter of Pisa; and the gay and debonair royal chaplain, Angilbert, recognized lover of the king's daughter Bertha. Charlemagne himself studied under his appointed schoolmasters subjects as varied as astronomy, lunar cycles, the tides, and viticulture. For his school he collected books and manuscripts from all over Europe and instructed his ambassadors to keep a ready eye and a ready purse for such materials whether of the church fathers or the great Latin classics. Besides collecting ancient texts, Charlemagne with Einhard's help assembled the ancient lays and epics of his race that had been handed down from one generation to another. These precious tribal memories were most unfortunately destroyed by his son and successor, the narrowly pious Louis.

Since the deposition of the last emperor of the West, the imperial idea, sustained within the Byzantine court at Constantinople, continued as a vague but still persistent afterimage of the West. Indeed during the firm reign of the Eastern emperor Justinian, his generals Belisarius and Narses had reconquered Italy and southern Spain, and the Eastern Empire loomed as the most potent force in the world. Pope John I had visited Constantinople in 525 to smooth over his differences with Justinian and the Eastern Church. But after Justinian the strength of the Byzantine Empire was sapped by the assaults of the Persians, the Avars, and the Arabs; and in the West, the Visigoths absorbed the empire's Spanish holdings, while the Lombards conquered northern Italy.

By the time of Charlemagne, the Byzantine Empire still maintained a shaky hold on southern Italy, although the papal see severed all relations with Byzantium in 781. In culture patterns as well as religion the Eastern Empire was becoming more remote, more incomprehensible to the West. Nevertheless, Charlemagne avoided any gesture of hostility toward Byzantium and the Byzantine possessions, even promising his eldest daughter Rothrud in marriage to the young Eastern Emperor Constantine VI, although for obscure reasons the betrothal was ultimately broken off.

Several years before this, Pope Adrian had died, and his successor, Leo III, an unworldly man of humble origins, was much resented by the aristocratic relations of the late pope. One afternoon on his way

to devotions Leo was set upon by a gang of hirelings, manhandled, and then hauled off to prison to be charged with perjury, venality, and adultery. Emissaries of Charlemagne who happened to be in Rome managed to rescue him and bring him back to Aachen. The king assured the pope that he would see justice done him. During the months of Pope Leo's Aachen sojourn the scholars of Charlemagne's court concerned themselves more and more with the idea of reviving the Empire of the West and with having the pope proclaim Charlemagne as the successor of the vanished line of Roman emperors.

In Rome the rebellion against Leo had been put down, and Charlemagne was able to send the pope back to Rome accompanied by a stout Frankish bodyguard capable of protecting him from any Roman faction. Those who had conspired against the pope now took their turn in prison. In that summer of the year 800, death came to Charlemagne's last wife, to whom for all his vagaries he was profoundly attached.

In August he informed his people that he was going to Rome to settle the case of the pope and punish the conspirators. A minor mutiny that had broken out in the Italian duchy of Benevento gave him the excuse for bringing a large army, led by his second son Pepin. Not until November did Charlemagne reach the Campagna, where he was met by Pope Leo with great ceremony fifteen miles north of Rome.

It took a month to hear the accusations and counter-accusations. Most of the noted theologians of the day were present at the vast assembly that decided the issue. The jailed conspirators were charged with slander, sacrilege, and violence. They in turn reiterated their accusations of perjury, venality, and adultery, although they were unable to produce one witness in confirmation. Looking beyond the immediate issue, the assembly unanimously ruled that none could sit in judgment on Christ's vicar. Those who had accused him were condemned to death, although on Charlemagne's intervention the sentence was modified to exile.

On December 23, in the Basilica of Saint Peter, Pope Leo stood in the pulpit clutching a book of the Gospels in his right hand, and solemnly swore "before God, the angels, and Saint Peter" that he was entirely innocent of all the charges against him. The next day, as if it were an omen, the envoy of the patriarch of Jerusalem arrived at Ostia bringing to Charlemagne the keys of the Church of the Holy

Bronze miniature of Charlemagne shows him in the peaceful attire of cloak and tunic. He rides without stirrups, then commonly used only in battle.

Sepulcher and the standard of Jerusalem. On Christmas morning the largest congregation ever to assemble within Saint Peter's gathered expectantly, for word had spread through Rome of the extraordinary event that was to take place that morning, nothing less than the resurrection of the Empire of the West in the person of the king of the Franks. To the very last, Charlemagne was hesitant, fearing not only trouble with Byzantium—which he wished to avoid—but that he might be scorned as a pretender, a usurper. At the pope's request he attended mass that morning wearing the tunic, purple and gold cloak, and jeweled sandals of a Roman patrician. There in the basilica, lighted by the waving glow of a thousand candles, he knelt in prayer, and as he rose Pope Leo stepped to his side and placed the imperial crown on his head. While he stood in silence those present shouted three times: "Life and victory to Charles Augustus, crowned by God, peace-loving and mighty Emperor of the Romans!" Then the pope with his attendants placed the cloak of imperial purple over the shoulders of the new Caesar Augustus.

Charlemagne ruled for fourteen years as emperor, years of peace which he spent in ordering and organizing his empire. He had divided Frankland into a number of regions known as Gaus, each ruled by a count who combined the functions of judge, chief constable, and military commander. The Gaus in turn were subdivided into administrative districts called "hundreds." No count was absolute in his Gau, for even the rank and file could appeal over his head to the crown, and he had no control over the religious houses within his territory. Furthermore, he was subject to inspection by the king's messengers, highly confidential officials who paid annual visits to all the Gaus and provinces.

An endless stream of capitularies issued from Aachen: regulations as to prices for basic commodities, tolls and taxes, repair of roads, and exports and imports; warnings to church officials; a veto on usury; even a law regulating a bride's dowry. Charlemagne established a royal mint with guaranteed standards for its coinage and forbade the previously private coinage of money. In place of the Roman system of direct taxation, he substituted a rendering of services to the state. He did not feel he could abolish the ancient custom of slavery, although he was uneasy about it and did his best to ease the slave's lot. He appointed a commission to revise the old Salic law, and introduced a "poor law" through which relief for the poor and dispossessed became for the first time obligatory. He laid down strict rules for Sabbath observances. Yet in spite of the minutiae of its regulations, his administration never degenerated into a frozen bureaucracy, and whatever its faults in a fallible world, it was a model for the future and a vast improvement on anything since the empire's fall.

For all his vision of a unified Christian Europe, Charlemagne in the end could not escape the legacy of his tribal past. The empire that he had assembled at the cost of so much blood and toil, he divided in his will among his three legitimate sons. To Charles, the eldest, went Frankland and the Saxon lands. Pepin, who from infancy had been king of Italy, received additionally Bavaria and Swabia. Louis, king of Aquitaine since the age of three, inherited Burgundy and the Spanish March. As yet Charlemagne had made no mention of who was to succeed him as emperor. If Charles and Pepin had not died several years before their father, the empire would probably have disintegrated at his death. Their deaths made him think of his own. In 813 he summoned his surviving son Louis to Aachen and had him crowned co-emperor. A year later, in January, 814, Charlemagne died, after a brief illness contracted when he returned from the hunt wet and shivering. He was buried beneath the altar of his own basilica. He was seventy-one years old.

"Of all the great rulers of men," wrote the Irish historian W. E. H. Lecky, "there has probably been no other who was so truly many-sided, whose influence pervaded so completely all the religious, intellectual and political modes of thought existing in his time." Inevitably he became a legend. By the millennial year 1000 the common folk of Europe were convinced that Charlemagne was not dead but asleep. So it was believed in Germany that the great emperor lay sleeping in a cave in Guddesberg in Hesse, that travelers would sometimes hear him ride by furiously on stormy nights, that in the country's great danger, he, Karl der Grosse, would come again to save his countrymen.

CHAPTER III

THE CAROLINGIAN EMPIRE SHATTERED

When King Louis of Aquitaine arrived at Aachen, his father was already in his grave. The new emperor had an arch of gold erected over the tomb with an inscription that reads, in part: BENEATH THIS LIES THE BODY OF CHARLES, GREAT AND DEVOUT EMPEROR, WHO NOBLY ENLARGED THE KINGDOM OF THE FRANKS.

Louis was the first to call himself Roman Emperor, assuming the title of Augustus that Charlemagne had refused to use. At his succession he was thirty-six years old, a gentle man for his day, genuinely religious, a scholar, who could compose verse in Latin, but who would prove too mild to restrain his counts and officials, too pious to control the clergy. Somewhat derisively he was nicknamed Le Débonnaire. After Charlemagne's tremendous personality, he seemed by inevitable contrast an uncertain figure although the memory of the great emperor would sustain him for several years. In his private life he was much more austere than his father, and one of his first acts was to reform the palace, purging it of its hangers-on, a number of whom happened to be his aunts. But he lacked energy. He failed to visit all the parts of the realm as his father had done, and took no steps to curb the counts

Scholarship, fostered by Charlemagne and his heirs, would continue to be an honored tradition in Germany. At left is Dürer's idealized scholar, Saint Jerome.

who, far from acting as servants of the emperor, were growing so independent that common people turned to them for protection rather than to the crown. Charlemagne's insignia—the crown and sceptre and sword—would remain, but the imperial power was oozing away. Vassal nobles with their fiefs, bishops and abbots with their benefices, would soon challenge the imperial authority as feudalism emerged.

Charlemagne had not been dead a dozen years when, as he had feared, the Vikings renewed their invasions, harassing the coastline and eventually moving up the Rhine, the Seine, and the Loire to devastate Frankish cities. Danish raiders struck as far as Paris and broke open the Carolingian ancestral tombs in the Abbey of Saint-Denis, then moving farther inland burned the Church of Saint Mary at Aachen. Saracens attacked and seized Sicily. Louis the Pious watched impotently. One of his first acts was to make his young sons Lothair and Pepin kings respectively of Bavaria and Aquitaine. He also confirmed his young nephew Bernard as king of Italy. Like his father he found himself caught in the conflict between the unity of the empire and the Frankish tradition of dividing the realm. In an effort to solve this dilemma Louis revoked his earlier scheme. In 817 he laid down the *Divisio imperii,* his formal division, by which his eldest son Lothair would share the title of emperor and become his father's administrative colleague. Pepin, in addition, received Gascony and the counties of Toulouse and Burgundy. Bavaria now went to the youngest son, Louis, who had been only an infant at the time of the earlier division. Each king was left to rule within his own dominions, but the emperor remained sovereign and the kings could neither marry, make war, nor conclude treaties without his consent. If they died leaving more than one son, there was to be no further division of the kingdom. At the death of Louis, the joint rule of the empire would revert to Lothair who would alone bear the title of emperor.

Practical events soon demonstrated the futility of such theoretical arrangements. One of the regulations of the *Divisio* was that after the emperor's death Italy would be subject to Lothair just as it had been to Louis and to Charlemagne. But King Bernard saw this inclusion as a threat to his own sovereignty and plotted with his advisers to overthrow Louis. It was an ill-supported revolt, soon put down by the Frankish counts who marched into Italy and brought Bernard back to

Aachen in chains. He was condemned to death, a sentence that Louis commuted to blindness. Bernard died a few days later from the effects of this treatment. It was an uncharacteristic act of cruelty for which Louis suffered such remorse that a year later he performed public penance at Attigny. However sincere, his gesture was nevertheless impolitic, undermining as it did the emperor's image of authority. His second impolitic act was to marry a Swabian princess, Judith, not long after the death of his first wife in 818. An attractive and intelligent if domineering young woman, Judith bore him a son in 823 whom he named Charles, and who is known to history as Charles the Bald. The *Divisio* of 817 had not reckoned with further additions to the royal heirs, and the remaining years of Louis' life are a chronicle of his efforts—abetted by Judith—to secure an inheritance for his last-born and the counterefforts of the elder sons to preserve the 817 decree.

In 829 the emperor, by an edict "issued of his own will," gave the six-year-old Charles part of Alemannia together with Alsace and Raetia and a segment of Burgundy. These regions had formed part of Lothair's portion, and he greatly resented the excision even though he was his half brother's godfather. At the court of Aachen, Bernard of Septimania had become the protector of the young Charles and soon grew to be the emperor's favorite courtier, entrusted with much of the administration of the imperial domain. Under Count Bernard's direction the partisans of Lothair were excluded from court, and Lothair himself ceased to be designated coemperor. (He had by this time succeeded to his cousin's throne in Italy where, it was apparently hoped, he could not interfere with events in Aachen.)

Louis' three older sons grew increasingly suspicious of Bernard and of Judith, whom they soon accused of adultery. Pepin, on hearing rumors that the emperor planned to strip him of his kingdom, joined with his brother Louis in a coup. The sons declared they had no quarrel with their father, but only with Judith and Bernard. The coup, staged in 830, was quick and almost bloodless, for the military and the high nobility ranged themselves with the rebels. Rather than attempt a futile resistance, the emperor surrendered himself and his wife, after having dispatched Bernard to the safety of Barcelona. Their father overcome, Pepin and Louis immured their stepmother in a convent.

Lothair, biding his time in Italy, now returned with the intention of taking command of all the rebellious forces and resuming the imperial title. His first effort was to try to persuade his father to enter a monastery, but Louis refused. Instead the deposed emperor secretly made approaches to his sons Pepin and Louis, promising them additional lands if they would abandon Lothair. Meanwhile a reaction was spreading in favor of the emperor as his scattered followers rallied to him. With the tacit support of his other sons, Louis soon felt strong enough to defy Lothair and to arrest a number of the rebels while recalling Judith and resuming his abandoned title. Lothair, his support slipping away, his followers imprisoned or exiled, was forced to yield and to accept the pardon that his father now offered. Pepin as a reward received from the emperor the districts between the Loire and the Seine, while Louis of Bavaria—to be known as Louis the German—was granted Saxony, Thuringia, and most of what is today Belgium and the Netherlands. Young Charles received Burgundy, Provence, and Gothia with the province of Reims.

In spite of their superficial accord, Pepin put off visiting his father at Aachen, and when he did he was received so coldly that he fled in alarm to Aquitaine, disregarding his father's prohibition against doing so. Emperor Louis was preparing to take strong measures against such recalcitrance when he found himself threatened by Louis the German who had led his Bavarians into Alemannia. The emperor, with a superior force of Franks and Saxons, forced his son to submit and to swear never again to revolt.

The seesaw pattern of revolt and counterrevolt was repetitive in its grimness. When in 832 the emperor, again reconciled to Lothair, marched against Aquitaine, Pepin hastily proffered his submission and surrendered his person. Held in captivity, he was snatched away by Aquitanian insurgents who had come to regard Pepin as their prince and were alarmed over indications that young Charles was to be their new lord. Louis left Aquitaine, his plans having failed, only to find his other two sons were again mutinous. As king of Italy, Lothair this time found an ally in the new pope, Gregory IV. Gregory crossed the Alps to join Lothair when he advanced to combine forces with those of Louis the German. Two hostile armies now threatened each other, though both sides seemed to prefer negotiation and intrigue to passage of arms. The sons as usual professed the deepest respect for their father, asserting that their only quarrel was with his evil councilors.

But when Louis prepared to confer with his sons near Colmar in Alsace, he discovered that, just as before, almost all his supporters had been suborned and that his army had melted away. In his impotence he had no alternative but to surrender, with Judith and the young Charles, to Lothair. Lothair triumphantly deposed his father and claimed the empire for himself. Louis the Pious was forced to make a public confession of guilt and to prostrate himself as a penitent before the altar of Notre Dame of Compiègne. Judith was sent under armed guard to Italy and young Charles to a monastery.

Once more Pepin and Louis the German looked with dubious envy at their brother's sudden imperial status. Once more they connived, summoned their followers, and marched, ostensibly to aid their father. Lothair in a quick, familiar turnabout found himself abandoned by his higher nobility and clergy, and in 834 was forced to capitulate ignominiously, restoring the imperial insignia to his father and freeing his stepmother and half brother. He was also forced to stay within the kingdom of Italy and never again cross the Alps without permission.

But even as the twice-restored Louis attempted to establish a degree of order in his uneasy realm, Scandinavian pirates were harassing the coast and rivers. Nor did the interval of peace prove durable. In spite of Lothair's previously traitorous conduct, the emperor reverted to his old plan of making the king of Italy the future protector of the young Charles. On learning of these negotiations, Louis the German made his own approach and his own offer to Lothair. When the emperor discovered this, he deprived Louis of all his territory except Bavaria. Meanwhile Lothair had recrossed the Alps with the emperor's consent, and father and son went through a solemn ceremony of reconciliation.

The problems of imperial succession at last seemed simplified by Pepin's death in 838. Pepin's son, Pepin II, was thrust aside, and Louis the Pious now divided the empire into two more or less equal parts, the eastern part going to Lothair and the west to Charles. On the father's death, Lothair as the eldest was to bear the title of emperor and on him would fall the obligation of protecting the young Charles. Louis the German was cut off with little more than Bavaria. The wayward Bavarian, following the familiar filial pattern, now took up arms against his father, launching an invasion of Saxony and Thuringia. This time the emperor found no great difficulty in repelling the threat, but during his return to Worms in June of 840 where he had again arranged to meet Lothair, he took ill and died, probably of pneumonia. Just before his death, he proclaimed Lothair emperor and dispatched to him the sceptre, crown, and sword of imperial authority while commending Judith and Charles to his protection. Then, as a last gesture, the dying man sent a pardon to his son Louis the German.

The turbulent reign of Louis the Pious with its intermittent rebellions was only a portent of what was to come when his three sons faced each other alone in the world. Lothair learned of his father's death while he was on his way to Worms and proceeded at once to Strasbourg where his nobles swore an oath of fealty to him. He at once claimed "the empire as it had been formerly intrusted to him," that is the settlement of 817 which subordinated his two brothers to his imperial authority. Louis the German and Charles the Bald did not see it that way. Louis, in response to Lothair's succession, sent his forces to the east border of the Rhine, while Charles quickly mobilized. The new emperor, unwilling to face this double challenge, arranged to meet his brothers at the palace of Attigny the following May. The three spent that winter enlisting supporters and gathering troops, but in the spring Lothair failed to appear at the agreed meeting. Charles and Louis, equally threatened by their brother's claims, joined their armies together and marched against the emperor. Lothair in turn was joined by the disinherited Pepin II who still retained strong support in Aquitaine. Louis and Charles sent embassy after embassy to Lothair begging him to "restore peace to the Church of God." Lothair, confident that his army was more than a match for his adversaries, replied haughtily that "the imperial dignity had been committed to him, and he would know how to fulfil the duties it laid upon him." The two armies met near the village of Fontenoy, north of Auxerre, in the bloodiest battle that had been seen in Europe in many decades. Lothair's imperial troops held the center firm against those of Louis the German, and Pepin II steadied the left wing. But Charles, with a reinforcement of Burgundians, finally carried the day by smashing Lothair's right wing. The emperor was forced to retreat, though with his forces intact and in good order. Some forty thousand men-at-arms were killed on that "accursed day" according to one chronicler, although his is undoubt-

Part of the equipage of a gentleman hunter of the Middle Ages: a carved ivory hunting horn used to summon his dogs and his bowmen

edly an exaggeration. Nevertheless, the slaughter was vast. The poet Angilbert wrote that "the garments of the slain Frankish warriors whitened the plain as birds usually do in the autumn."

Yet bloody though the Battle of Fontenoy had been, long lingering in the folk memory, it was not decisive. Lothair in the security of Aachen soon refurbished his army, and after his brothers had gone their separate ways he marched against Louis and was diverted only when Charles marched against him. In the face of this persisting imperial threat, Charles and Louis met in Strasbourg, there taking a solemn oath to support one another in any crisis. Each took the oath in the language of his allies, Louis in the Romance tongue, Charles in German. Together they condemned what they called Lothair's crime in failing to recognize the judgment of God in the defeat at Fontenoy, and a month later they advanced their combined armies against the emperor. Lothair retreated, abandoning Aachen without a struggle. In the course of the retreat his army was swept by mass desertions and he was forced to sue for peace terms which were finally embodied in a treaty at Verdun in 843. By this treaty, which repartitioned the Carolingian empire into three parts, Lothair, while retaining his now empty title of emperor, received the thousand-mile-long Middle Kingdom—Italy plus a narrow strip running from Italy through Aachen to the North Sea that included Provence, Burgundy, and Lorraine. Louis kept his essentially Germanic realm, that is the Eastern Kingdom, while Charles ruled over the Romance-speaking lands that roughly corresponded to medieval France. Although nationality had not yet emerged as a concept, although each king had disparate tribal and racial mixtures within his kingdom, the Treaty of Verdun nevertheless drew the outline, set the pattern for modern France and Germany, while Burgundy lying in between would remain to be disputed as a border region long after it had vanished as an entity.

The disorganization of the Carolingian Empire and the weakness of the contending kings brought their inevitable counterbalance in the rise of feudalism. After the empire had split into three kingdoms, the kingdoms themselves lapsed into a multitude of duchies and counties whose dukes and counts, while maintaining a theoretical allegiance to their kings, became within their own domains virtually independent rulers with the power of conscripting, taxing, and judging their vassals, subjects, and fiefs. When the power of the crown could no longer protect against external and internal disorder, the small man transferred his allegiance to the great man, yielding up his land and receiving it back with the lord's protection in return for defined services. Out of such mutual obligations, extended in pyramidal form through society, feudalism arose. During the same period the foot soldier was giving way to cavalry, partly as a result of the innovation of stirrups and iron horseshoes. The old Germanic levy had been self-sufficient, freemen obeying the summons of the king. The new armed horseman, the knight, with his retainers, was so costly to furnish and maintain in the field that only a manor could sustain him. Counts provided the knights, forging another link of dependency in the feudal chain.

Under Charlemagne's rule the counts had been his appointed officers subject to his approval and disapproval, with no tenure beyond the emperor's pleasure. Grants of land remained his means of rewarding them and other faithful servants, grants that for the most part did not extend beyond the life of the holder. But with Charlemagne's passing, the title and the land had come to be hereditary. Benefices, granted to laymen and ecclesiasts for life, evolved into hereditary fiefs. No land without a lord, it came to be said. The chain of vassalage ran from the count, nominally the king's vassal, to the baron, to the lord of the manor and the knight, and then to the villein, the peasant, the tiller of the soil in whose sweat-stained person the chain ended. Slavery as an institution gradually gave way to villeinage in which the villein was at least a person, while a slave had been a thing. Most peasants were attached to the land, subject to their lord's jurisdiction and whim, protected within their harsh existence rather by custom than by law.

Charlemagne had abolished the tribal dukedoms, but with the disintegration of the empire under his successors, the tribes again turned to their hereditary chiefs, and these in ruling their territory as a duchy resurrected the title of duke. In Germany the unity imposed by the Frankish conquest broke down as the four duchies of Saxony, Bavaria, Swabia, and Franconia reasserted themselves, while across the Rhine the duchy of Lorraine would long remain an object of contention between the rulers of the Eastern and Western Frankish kingdoms.

With Louis the Pious' death Lothair became emperor, but it was an empty title and any attempt he made to assume authority met with hostility from his brothers. In spite of their agreements to meet frequently and assist one another, they continued to intrigue. Charles the Bald's authority in Aquitaine had never been wholly assured, and when the disaffected nobles sent envoys to Louis the German offering him the Aquitanian throne, he agreed to send his son Louis the Younger as king. The plan was frustrated by Charles' alliance with Lothair and by the reappearance of Pepin II, to whom the nobles rallied rather than to Louis the Younger.

In 855, the fifteenth year of his reign, the weary emperor retired to an abbey, where he died shortly after dividing the Middle Kingdom among his three sons. To Louis II went Italy and the imperial title, Lothair II received the region which would henceforth bear his name—Lotharingia, or Lorraine—and Charles the Younger, a feeble epileptic, became king of Provence. Louis the German attempted a *rapprochement* with Lothair II but the nephew refused to be tempted from the alliance with Charles the Bald that his father had made.

Aquitaine again became an issue in the summer of 858 when the disaffected nobles, taking advantage of the absence of Lothair II on a joint campaign with his uncle Charles against the Vikings, again appealed to Louis the German, who this time marched across Alsace to that uneasy kingdom. However, the carnage of Fontenoy had given the Frankish counts as well as the kings a permanent distaste for indiscriminate bloodshed. Charles and Louis opened negotiations, and in this maneuvering the astute German managed to suborn most of his half brother's vassals. Charles, when he realized his weakness, retreated to Burgundy while Louis proclaimed himself king of the Western Kingdom and proceeded to deal out honors and benefices to the nobles whose allegiance he had subverted.

By January, 859, Charles had rallied enough supporters to feel free to march against Louis the German. Louis, surprised in this advance, found himself deserted by most of his nobles and retreated to Germany. More bloodless negotiations followed, culminating in a shipboard meeting of the two brothers in the middle of the Rhine. Eventually they came to an agreement, sworn to in both languages, which was essentially a return to the *status quo* before Louis's invasion.

Meanwhile Lothair II, who had been compelled by his father to marry against his will, was bending all his efforts to get rid of his childless wife in order to marry his mistress. The prospect was intriguing. If Lothair should die childless, his uncles could be expected to take over Lorraine, since Louis II was far away in Italy and the epileptic Charles the Younger close to death. Charles the Bald, backed by the powerful archbishop of Reims, thus opposed his nephew's matrimonial vagaries as did Louis the German who, after some wavering, met his half brother at Tusey, where in 865 they renewed their oath of peace and friendship. Lothair, after several unsuccessful attempts to divest himself of his wife, made a visit to Pope Adrian II in August, 869, in an effort to persuade him to grant the annulment denied by the previous pope. Returning with Adrian's promise to reopen the case, the king of Lorraine was taken ill and died.

Disregarding the awkward promises of earlier treaties, Charles the Bald at once marched an army into Lorraine and in September, 869, had himself crowned king of Lothair's realm. Louis the German in his turn collected his forces and advanced on Lorraine while calling on his brother to give up the seized territory. Once more two Carolingian armies confronted each other, and once more talk took the place of combat. Louis and Charles, meeting at Mersen on the banks of the Meuse, amicably divided up Lothair II's possessions, splitting the sources of revenue equably and paying no attention at all to linguistic or natural boundaries. Both kings found themselves recalled from their division of the spoils by family dissension. Charles was forced to return to the Western Kingdom and put down a revolt by his son Carloman, whose brashness he punished by having his eyes put out. Two of Louis the German's three sons had unsuccessfully revolted against him, though with consequences much less devastating to themselves.

The kings' ambitions and cupidity were once more aroused by the death of the king-emperor in Italy. Charles again got there first, arriving with his army to be welcomed by the pope, who saw him as the champion of the Holy See against the Saracens ensconced in the south of Italy. Louis the German dispatched his two sons, Charles the Fat and a second Carloman, with an army across the Alps, while he himself invaded Lorraine. But Charles the Fat turned back almost before he started, and Carloman when he finally confronted his uncle Charles the Bald, allowed himself to be outnegotiated and outmaneuvered, and returned from Italy without winning a concession or striking a blow.

Charles the Bald went to Rome where he received the imperial crown from the pope and recognition as king of Italy. On learning this, Louis the German sent envoys angrily demanding an equable division of the Italian territories. The new emperor dispatched a conciliatory embassy to his brother, but shortly after, Louis the German died.

According to Frankish custom and to Louis's wishes, his kingdom was divided among his sons. Carloman received Bavaria; Louis the Younger, Saxony and Franconia; and Charles the Fat, Alemannia. Charles the Bald immediately laid claim to that portion of Lorraine deeded to his brother at Mersen and set out with an army to reinforce his claim. Louis of Saxony, as Louis the German's son was henceforth known, sent peace envoys to his uncle, while at the same time crossing the Rhine in force to encamp at Andernach. Charles, in the midst of preliminary negotiations, secretly prepared a surprise attack that he hoped would overwhelm his nephew. After an exhausting all-night march in the autumn rain, he arrived with his army at Louis's camp just before daybreak. Louis had been warned and his forces were on the alert. Charles' assault turned into a disaster. His soldiers were repulsed and then routed. Louis took much booty and many prisoners but lacked the strength to follow up his victory. The following year, in spite of Viking inroads and the dubious loyalty of his chief vassals, Charles left for Rome to aid the pope in his struggle against the Saracens. On the return journey he suddenly died, poisoned, it was said, by his own physician.

With the death of Charles the Bald, the empire of Charlemagne, beset by Vikings and threatened by powerful independent nobles from within, drifted from decline into confusion and anarchy. Charles was succeeded by his son Louis the Stammerer who as king of the Western Franks concluded a treaty with his German cousins partitioning Lothair's Lorraine. At his death a year later a group of disaffected nobles persuaded Louis of Saxony to invade from the West and challenge the joint inheritance of Louis the Stammerer's young sons, Louis III and Carloman. The Saxon king reached Verdun, but, on failing to receive the expected support from the Western Frankish nobles, withdrew. A second invasion attempt on his part met with similar results.

When in the year 882 Charles the Fat held a conference with his cousins Louis III and Carloman, the three kings agreeing to combine

Charles the Bald, who outfought and outmaneuvered his kin to gain the imperial throne, is shown receiving a Bible in this manuscript illumination.

their forces to deal with rebellious Provence. This successful campaign was interrupted when Charles, at the frantic urgings of the pope, hurried to Italy to protect the Holy See against the ravages of the dukes of Spoleto. There, as a reward for his help, Charles was crowned emperor, but soon after returned to Germany to take possession of Saxony, inherited on the death of his brother Louis. Two years earlier Charles the Fat had acquired Bavaria after the death of his brother. With Saxony added to his possessions he now became ruler of the whole Eastern Kingdom. Nor would his rule end there, for in the Western Kingdom Louis III had died of a fall from a horse, and sixteen months later, in 884, his brother Carloman was killed in a hunting accident. Since Louis the Stammerer's third son was too young to reign, the Frankish nobles offered the vacant throne to Charles the Fat.

Once more the kingdoms of Charlemagne's empire were united under a single ruler. But the new emperor lacked the domineering personality and active vigor of the first emperor, even as he lacked the manpower and resources. The Vikings were pressing on from their now permanent base in Flanders. Revolts broke out among his subjects, were suppressed and then succeeded by new revolts. Finally after Charles had been emperor for three years, his nobles turned against him and at the end of 887 deprived him of his throne. The following January he died. His deposition by his own nobles marked the final disintegration of the Carolingian Empire, and so it was understood even by contemporaries. "The kingdoms which had been subject to the government of Charles split up into fragments," a chronicler wrote, "breaking the bond which united them, and without waiting for their natural lord, each one sought to create a king of its own, drawn from within itself, which thing was a cause of long wars. . . ." The abstract idea of empire receded into the background, giving way to the blood attachment of race and native soil. The Western Franks now elected as their king Count Odo, the valiant defender of Paris against the Vikings; in Italy Guy, duke of Spoleto, and Berengar I, marquis of Friuli, contended for the crown; the son of the count of Auxerre claimed Lorraine; Louis of Provence pushed his realm to the valley of the Rhone, while Count Boso of Provence had already before Charles' death founded the kingdom of Burgundy.

The insurgent vassals, after removing Charles the Fat, proclaimed

Count Arnulf of Carinthia (the illegitimate son of Carloman of Bavaria) the deposed emperor's successor; he seemed the leader best suited by his warlike qualities to defend the tottering empire or at least to defend Germany. Arnulf was recognized by the proliferating kinglets as at least a theoretical overlord, while he himself nursed the dream of gaining the imperial crown. Only distrust of his nobles prevented him from leaving at once for Italy. There the marquis of Friuli and the duke of Spoleto continued their intermittent struggle that climaxed in a bloody battle in which Guy emerged victorious. He was named king, and then crowned emperor of the West by the reluctant but politic Pope Stephen V. Seven months later Stephen died, and his successor, Formosus, who distrusted Guy and feared an Italian emperor, appealed to Arnulf to cross the Alps and "restore order." After two abortive attempts, Arnulf finally arrived in Italy to find Guy dead and Guy's son Lambert installed as his successor. So hostile was the population to this German expeditionary force, despite the pope's good wishes, that Arnulf was forced to take Rome by direct assault. Formosus then crowned him emperor in the Basilica of Saint Peter. Because of his failing health the new emperor returned almost at once to Germany. No sooner had he crossed the Alps than Lambert again resumed the royal power.

Arnulf died in 899, leaving as heir his six-year-old son, Louis the Child, who in February, 900, was proclaimed by an assembly of Frankish nobles Louis III, king of Germany. Later he was also named titular head of Lorraine. Events swirled around the head of the hapless boy-king: civil war in Lorraine; a feud between the rival Franconian ducal houses of Conradin and Babenberg; and, most devastating of all, the incursions of bands of Hungarian horsemen. Arnulf had brought in this wandering Finnish folk to aid him in his war against the Moravians. Afterward the Hungarians established themselves permanently on the banks of the Tisza, and from there not a year passed without their raids into Germany. In 901 they swept across Carinthia, and a few years later ravaged Saxony, Thuringia, and Swabia. Finally in 910 they defeated the army sent against them by Louis the Child.

The following year Louis died. He was barely eighteen. With his passing, the rule of the Carolingians in Germany came to an end.

1526

CHAPTER IV

SAXON AND SALIAN RULERS

Upon the death of Louis the Child in 911, the Frankish, Saxon, Alemannian, and Bavarian nobles met at Forchheim to elect Conrad, duke of Franconia, as their king. Through his mother a grandson of the emperor Arnulf, Conrad was a valorous man thrust into a position of weakness. Never would he have sufficient resources to deal with the tribal dukes. In three expeditions he was unable to drive Charles the Simple from Lorraine. Continually he found himself faced with the ravages of the Hungarians, and the restiveness of his most powerful vassals often turned to outright revolt. Duke Arnulf of Bavaria flouted Conrad's authority at will, while the king's most powerful vassal, Duke Henry of Saxony, showed his hostility from the first. In 915, four years after Conrad's election, Henry came out in open rebellion. Yet three years later when Conrad was dying, he recognized the dominance of his old enemy. "The future of the realm," the king declared, "lies with the Saxons," and he ordered the royal insignia conveyed to the Saxon Duke Henry.

The nobles confirmed Conrad's choice and the leadership of Germany fell to the tribe that had against the greatest resistance entered

One of a series of tempera studies of native plants and flowers by Dürer, this one depicting the columbine

the Frankish Empire. Henry the Fowler, the new king would be called, because the messengers who brought the news of his election found him out hawking. Henry was the first of the Saxon kings and emperors who would endure for the next 105 years. His limited goal was to be king of a confederated Germany in which the administration of the duchies remained in the hands of the dukes. Arnulf the Bad, duke of Bavaria, had wanted the throne for himself, and Henry was forced to launch two campaigns against this stubborn vassal before Arnulf would recognize his authority.

Henry was determined to bring Lorraine back into the German realm, and taking advantage of civil war in France he thrice led an army across the Rhine, finally securing in 925 the allegiance of Duke Gilbert of Lorraine who then received Henry's daughter Gerberga in marriage. King Henry was much concerned with protecting Saxony and Thuringia from the ravages of the Hungarians and the incursions of the Slavic Wends. By the lucky capture of a Hungarian chief, he was able to demand as ransom that the Hungarians withdraw from Saxony and keep the peace for nine years. He used that time to strengthen his border garrisons and to build such fortified towns as Goslar and Bad Gandersheim. He reorganized his army, replacing foot soldiers with mounted men, and after four years of effort captured Brandenburg, long held by the Slavic Wends, forcing them to pay him an annual tribute. Even the troublesome Danes were then compelled to submit to him.

Henry had always remained cool to the claims of the Church, holding ecclesiastical authority at arm's length and steadily refusing a ritual coronation, although in his last years he founded a church and a nunnery in his favored residence of Quedlinburg. In 935 while hunting he was brought down by a paralyzing stroke. Near death, he summoned an assembly of nobles and had his second son, Otto, proclaimed his successor.

Even among contemporaries Henry the Fowler was recognized as the founder of a new realm and a new dynasty. Yet for all his accomplishments as statesman, soldier, and benevolent ruler, he was at most a prelude to his son, Otto the Great. Unlike his father the young and vigorous Otto regarded the royal power as a potency to be asserted. His model was Charlemagne's empire, his goal to fortify the central government and restore the imperial title. Instead of avoiding a coronation, he insisted on being crowned and anointed in symbolic Aachen. After the ceremony, to emphasize the union of the German tribes as the foundation of his rule, he had his dukes officiate at a state banquet —Eberhard of Franconia as steward, Hermann of Swabia as cupbearer, Arnulf of Bavaria as marshal, and Gilbert of Lorraine as chamberlain.

Otto realized that it was essential for him to use the resources of the Church to counteract the entrenched power of the dukes. His means were: lay investiture, through which he controlled the election of the higher clergy; the assertion of proprietary rights over many bishoprics and abbeys; and finally, the system of advocacy in which he appointed similar managers over the estates of cathedrals and monasteries. Many of the higher clergy he used as royal administrators. On these foundations he built up his wealth and military strength. At the beginning of his reign, the king left the administration of Saxony to the counts whom he appointed. When the hereditary dukes discovered that Otto regarded them as subordinate vassals, they soon were up in arms. After Duke Arnulf's death his sons refused to pay homage, and it took the king two campaigns in Bavaria to establish his authority there. Duke Eberhard, made bold by Otto's toleration of his raids on the Saxon borders, became even bolder and entered into a conspiracy with Otto's younger brother Henry to overthrow him, a conspiracy that was soon joined by Duke Gilbert. When civil war broke out in Lorraine, Otto hastened with his army to put it down, but while crossing the Rhine near Xanten his advance guard was ambushed by the conspirators. Although outnumbered, the royal troops succeeded in outflanking the enemy in a swift double-envelopment movement that carried the day. Otto, watching from across the river, viewed his victory as "a miracle of God" and attributed it to the Holy Lance which he held in his hand. Whatever the reason, the conspiracy was broken. Henry fled, and was allowed by his lenient brothers to leave Saxony unharmed.

The ensuing peace was short. That same year, 939, Gilbert again rebelled, this time with the support of the new king of France, Louis IV, "d'Outremer," who secretly planned to attach Lorraine to his realm. Henry once more joined Gilbert, as did Eberhard. Otto's cause seemed lost, until in a brief skirmish near Andernach Gilbert and Eberhard were both killed. The isolated Henry fled, then threw himself on his brother's mercy and was pardoned. Otto's persistent magnanimity, however, did not prevent Henry from plotting his brother's assassination two years later. This abortive plot was discovered and Henry again fled, was captured, and imprisoned. Yet before the year's end the king pardoned him.

In restoring order to his kingdom Otto took care to grant the vacant dukedoms to members of his own family whenever he did not—as in the case of Franconia—retain them for himself. When the duke of Bavaria died, Otto replaced him with Henry, who from a persistent rebel now became one of the king's most loyal subjects. The duke of Swabia's death gave Otto the further opportunity of presenting that duchy to his own son Liudolf.

Taking advantage of Germany's internal problems, Wends and Hungarians, Slavs and Danes, once more threatened the borders. Lorraine remained a troubled, uncertain area between evolving France and Germany. Otto and Louis d'Outremer finally were able to settle their differences over this province, but the new duke of Lorraine, Conrad, continued to nurse grievances.

Meanwhile, Otto watched with both interest and concern as the Lombard kingdom of Italy disintegrated. King Lambert had been succeeded by Berengar of Friuli, grandson on his mother's side of Louis the Pious. King Berengar I was a devious man who though never in control of his nobles nevertheless received the imperial crown from the hated soldier-pope, John X. Since Lambert's time the emperor had come to be regarded as little more than a protector of the pope. The crown became a bauble, a counter between the "Pornocracy"—as the papacy was then known—and a corrupt and decadent nobility. In 924, nine years after his coronation, Berengar was murdered. In 926, with the connivance and encouragement of Pope John, Duke Hugh of Provence—a strong, if wily, ruler—came to Italy to claim the Lombard throne as a descendant of the house of Lothair. He was crowned king, and expected to be crowned emperor, but before this latter event could take place Pope John too was murdered.

The greatest remaining Italian chief, Berengar of Ivrea, nephew of the murdered Berengar I, continued to threaten Hugh's rule. When Berengar learned that Hugh was planning to seize and blind him, he fled to the court of Otto the Great where he continued to plot against

A twelfth-century manuscript illustration portraying the election ceremonies at which the emperor was chosen.

Hugh. In the winter of 945 Berengar returned to Italy and rallied the nobles and great prelates to him. So massive was the defection from King Hugh that he finally sent his far more popular son, Lothair II, to gather support. Berengar, fearing that Hugh was withdrawing only to plot a later invasion, agreed to accept Lothair as king and further decided to reinstate Hugh as a nominal coruler. Two years later Hugh again abdicated and retired to Provence.

With the young Lothair on the throne, Berengar ruled as "chief councilor of the realm." A weak, greedy man, and like the first Berengar unable to control his nobles, he nevertheless on the death of Lothair II in 950 was able to secure his election and that of his son Adalbert as joint kings. Opposition to the house of Berengar now centered in Lothair's widow, the beautiful though childless Adelaide, whom Berengar seized and imprisoned, confiscating her properties. Managing to escape, she appealed to Otto for protection.

Otto had long dreamed of reviving Arnulf's empire and establishing himself as the suzerain of Western Christendom. Adelaide's appeal brought him over the Brenner Pass with an army. The Italian churchmen and most of the nobility flocked to his side, and Berengar fled. Not only did Otto rescue Adelaide but—being a romantically minded widower—he married her. Having bloodlessly conquered half the kingdom of which he now assumed the title, Otto returned to Germany leaving his son-in-law Duke Conrad of Lorraine behind with his army. He failed however in his more fundamental goal, for Pope Agapetus, a partisan of Berengar, refused to crown him emperor.

Scarcely had Otto arrived back in Germany before Conrad and Berengar came to terms, terms which gave Berengar practically a free hand in Italy. Otto, preoccupied with internal revolts and frontier wars, let events beyond the Alps take their course. When the Hungarians again invaded Germany, they were aided and encouraged by Conrad and Otto's son Liudolf, the duke of Swabia. Otto drove off the Hungarians, put down the revolt, and deprived Conrad and Liudolf of their dukedoms. He now stabilized his kingdoms by filling the vacant duchies, as well as the bishoprics of Mainz, Cologne, and Trier, with trustworthy friends and relatives. When the Hungarians again threatened, he felt sufficiently secure to march a vast army against them. Carrying the victorious banner of Saint Michael, he met the massed

Hungarians at Lechfeld near Augsburg and so routed and destroyed the Magyar army that the broken survivors were never again a menace to Germany. The Battle of Lechfeld fought in August, 955, was one of the decisive events of history, bringing security to the West from the ominous and persistent threats of Hungarian hordes.

By 960 Otto had finally established his rule and his fame as Europe's most powerful monarch. Envoys from Rome, Greece, Russia, and even Arabia visited his court bringing gifts of gold and silver and ivory and spices, and such unfamiliar animals as lions, camels, monkeys, and ostriches. When the dissolute boy-pope John XII, grandson of the duke of Spoleto, found his territories ravaged by Berengar and Adalbert, he appealed to Otto for help, promising him in return the imperial crown. What had been previously denied, Otto now saw as attainable, and rallying an army he once again crossed the Brenner Pass, putting Berengar to flight and reaching Rome without resistance. On February 2, 962, with Adelaide by his side, he was crowned in Saint Peter's by Pope John, his swordbearer standing ominously by during the ceremony with drawn sword. Otto had achieved his goal as the revived Roman emperor of the West, Charlemagne's successor. To the pope he promised protection and the restoration of alienated papal lands. John and the Romans swore allegiance to his person and agreed to the revival of the Carolingian pact by which papal elections were subject to imperial confirmation.

Pope John, now a subject, soon wearied of his subordinate state and plotted against Otto. On discovering this, Otto, then in pursuit of Berengar, returned hastily to Rome. John having fled, Otto presided over the synod which deposed the pope for gross misconduct and elected a layman, Leo VIII, as his successor. While Otto was occupied with a campaign that made a prisoner of Berengar, John with his supporters was able to oust Leo, who barely escaped with his life. Before Otto could move against John, the latter died. Though the Romans tried to assert their independence by electing a learned and saintly Benedict V, Otto forced him from the papal throne and reinstated his puppet Leo. And when Leo died, the Romans in obedience to Otto elected John XIII, then rose against their forced choice and restored him only after Otto undertook a third Italian expedition. Otto's goal in this expedition was to occupy the southern Italian possessions of the

Byzantine Empire. After an indecisive campaign that ended in a stalemate, Otto agreed to negotiate with the Eastern emperor, who recognized Otto's Western rule and sent the Greek princess Theophano as a bride for Otto's son, Otto II.

After his son's marriage in Rome, Otto the Great returned to Germany, where he died the following year, his work complete. His reign had ushered in a revival of stable government, commerce, and civilization following the anarchic collapse of Charlemagne's empire. He had brought into existence the Romano-Germanic Empire of the West that would later be known as the Holy Roman Empire. From his time on only German kings would wear the imperial crown. During his reign Germans had grown increasingly conscious of themselves as members of a nation rather than members of a tribe. The word *German,* which had meant only a language, now came to mean a country and a people as well.

For better or for worse, Otto had brought about the union of Germany and northern Italy, and the fate of both lands would for centuries derive from this achievement. For better because through his Italian kingdom he had brought Germany into contact with a higher civilization and had given that limited region access to the commercial highways of the world. For worse because generations of Germans would shed their blood on Italian battlefields, while emperors with distant aims would fail in the more immediate one of uniting the German people into one nation.

Otto II was barely eighteen when his father died, although he had already been crowned coemperor in his father's lifetime. The usual disorders followed the accession of the new monarch, and for five years Otto was kept in Germany by the revolt of his ambitious cousin, Duke Henry the Wrangler of Bavaria, by risings in Lorraine, and by the invasion of Saxony by Harold Bluetooth, king of Denmark. Having at last secured his frontiers, Otto II set out for Italy, anxious to succeed where his father had failed. The Italian territories of the Eastern Empire, weakened by civil strife in Byzantium, had been subject to increasing Saracen raids, and Otto expected Greek officials to welcome his overlordship and join in repelling the heathen. They, however, in spite of his Byzantine wife, despised him as a barbarian and refused to give aid. Allied with them, the German emperor might have swept the peninsula clear of the Saracens. Opposed by them and with little military capacity of his own, he was soon routed by a Saracen army and barely managed to escape with his life. He died in Italy the following year while trying to raise a new army for another campaign against the south, and was buried in Rome's Saint Peter's in 983.

Before Otto's death the German nobles had already elected his son, Otto III, as king, although at his succession he was only three years old. News of Otto's Italian disaster spread rapidly through Germany and northern Europe and stirred up the restive heathen tribes. Danes overran the Danish March, and between the Elbe and the Oder the Slavs laid waste Otto the Great's episcopal towns and churches. Then in a sudden coup Henry the Wrangler seized the person of the young king and made himself regent after having the child crowned in Aachen. It was a position he could not sustain after the leading nobles of Saxony, Swabia, Franconia, and Lorraine united against him, and in return for the safe tenure of his own duchy of Bavaria he surrendered both king and regency to the boy's mother.

As the king's guardian for the next decade, Theophano preserved the realm intact, ruling with skill and resolution. Yet she could not overcome her inherited feeling that Germany was barbarous. The boy king, part Greek, part Italian, and only part German, grew up with contempt for his native Saxony and with the conviction that the Italian kingdom was more important than Germany, that Italy was his true home. At fourteen he became king in his own right. His seven-year reign was only an interlude, but this dreamy, visionary, and religious young man so dazzled his contemporaries that they remembered him as the "Wonder of the World." At first content to compare himself with Charlemagne, he later saw himself as the successor of Constantine, the Christian renewer of the old Roman Empire. When Pope John XV appealed to him for help against the Roman nobility, he marched with a great army for Italy. Since John died before Otto reached Rome, the sixteen-year-old king was able to install his 24-year-old cousin Bruno on the papal throne as Gregory V, the first German to become pope. The new pope then crowned his cousin as emperor and Otto returned to his favored German residence, Charlemagne's Aachen.

Otto regarded himself as an apostle, a Pauline "servant of Jesus Christ" as much as an emperor. In the millennial year 1000 he made a

long pilgrimage to various shrines, accompanied by Roman nobles and cardinals. Pausing at Charlemagne's tomb, he had it opened to gaze at his great predecessor, whom he found sitting upright in death, a golden crown on his head and a sceptre in his hands. On Otto's return to Rome a revolt broke out which he could not quell with the forces at his command, and he was obliged to retreat to Ravenna. There he briefly considered abandoning the world to become a monk. But the feeling for his imperial mission and the desire for vengeance proved stronger than his ascetic impulse, and he was preparing to march on Rome with reinforcements that had just arrived from Germany when he was taken mortally ill of smallpox.

Otto III left no heirs. What he did leave was a tottering realm, the foundations of which had been so undermined that it would take the best efforts of his successors, Henry II and Conrad II, to shore them up. In 1002 with some hesitancy the nobles elected Duke Henry of Bavaria, son of Henry the Wrangler, cousin of Otto, and the great-grandson of Henry the Fowler, as king. Henry II was a pious, upright man

Personifications of the Slavic lands, Germany, Gaul, and Rome are shown bearing offerings to their new emperor Otto III.

of great dignity, so devout that after his death he and his wife Kunigunde would be canonized. A practical man for all his religiosity, far more aware of the possible than his dreamy predecessor, he lacked capacity as a military commander and suffered from continual bad health. Though he would undertake three expeditions to Italy, he remained chiefly concerned with Germany, regarding the kingdom to the south as a "harlot land." "Restoration of the Empire of the Franks" was the motto he had engraved on his seal. Devoted to law and order, zealous in suppressing ecclesiastical abuses, he traveled untiringly across his realm, overseeing officials and dispensing justice. His concern with the Church and his efforts to reform it were constant.

In comparison with Otto the Great, Henry's hold over the secular nobles was weak. There would not be any combined rising against him, but there would be many lesser intrigues. In his campaigns against the suddenly formidable Polish state, Henry was uniformly unsuccessful, the Poles advancing as far as the Elbe, although in the end he did retrieve Bohemia for the empire. Before he could be crowned king of

Otto, flanked by clerics and warriors, holds court. His orb signifies the earth; his staff symbolizes his divinely inspired right to rule.

Italy, the Lombards revolted and enthroned Ardoin, marquis of Ivrea. However, Ardoin was a man of such violent and overbearing nature that the other Italian nobles soon begged Henry to intervene. Henry's first expedition to Italy in 1004 found most of Ardoin's supporters ready to desert to the German, and Ardoin was driven from Pavia without resistance. Afterward, however, a furious quarrel broke out between the townsmen and Henry's soldiers in which the Germans looted the city and burned it to the ground, a horror the Italians would not forget for generations. Eight years later, when rival popes disputed the papal throne, Henry again intervened and late in 1013 marched to Italy accompanied by his queen and a number of German bishops. The following February, he entered Rome to be met at the door of Saint Peter's by one of the contenders, Benedict VIII. That martial pope, in return for Henry's pledge of support, anointed and crowned him emperor.

Henry's second Italian expedition insured the continuity of the Western Empire, renewing the alliance with the papacy and re-establishing the German monarchy as foremost in western Europe. His third and final expedition, in 1022, was at the urging of Pope Benedict, who now found himself threatened by the advancing Byzantines. Henry launched a campaign successful enough to check the Greeks and insure the safety of Rome, but was forced to call a halt after his army was stricken with the plague. In Rome emperor and pope collaborated on ecclesiastical reforms that did much to revive the strength and stature of the papacy. Both Benedict and Henry had only two more years to live. The last of the Saxon emperors died childless. He was entombed in his own cathedral of Bamberg, the see that he himself had founded.

On Henry's death the princes elected the son of Count Henry of Speyer, chiefly because his great-grandmother had been the daughter of Otto the Great, although they were undoubtedly influenced by his energy and military skill. He became Conrad II and with him began the Salian or Franconian line of emperors that would rule Germany for the next century. Unlike most such occasions, his election was a festive event without tumult or dissension. Eight days later, on September 4, 1024, he was crowned at Mainz. In his fifteen-year reign Conrad further consolidated the imperial power in Germany. While enlarging his empire, he took great care not to overextend himself. He drove the Poles back across the Oder and sealed his friendship with King Canute of Denmark and England by marrying his son to Canute's daughter. In Italy he leagued himself with the lay princes in the north; in the south he made alliances with the Normans who had come to that region as mercenaries and pirates and had remained to rule.

The Italian nobles were bitterly divided in their allegiance to their new German overlord. Not until after a revolt had been put down there did Conrad venture into Italy. Then, appearing in Rome on Easter, 1027, before a vast gathering of Italian and German princes, he was crowned emperor by Pope John XIX, a coronation marred afterward by street rioting between Romans and foreigners.

Conrad did his best to pacify and consolidate Italy. He encouraged the intermarriage of Italian and German princely houses and he appointed Germans to vacant Italian bishoprics. Ten years after his coronation, the great Italian nobles were in bitter dispute with their vassals—the vavasors and knights—whose positions had not been established as hereditary; both parties appealed to the emperor to mediate. "If Italy hungers for law, I will satisfy her," he remarked as he prepared another expedition south. Just as Conrad's sympathies and support had been with the small tenants in Germany, so in Italy he favored the lesser vassals. In his decree of 1037, one of the most important in feudal law, he ruled that fiefs were hereditary and that "no vassal of a bishop, abbot, abbess, marquis, count, or anyone holding an imperial or ecclesiastical fief" could be deprived of it except by the judgment of his peers. On the way back from Italy Conrad's army was struck by pestilence. He himself contracted the disease, and though he survived, he never recovered strength. Conrad died the following year. Long before his death he had resolved to supplant the ancient German tradition of monarchic election by the hereditary principle, and with this in mind he had designated his son Henry as successor when the boy was only nine years old, and had taken care to have his choice ratified by the German princes.

Henry III (called Henry the Black), who was crowned king at Aachen in 1028 and assumed full powers in 1039 at the age of twenty-two, led the Holy Roman Empire to a peak of greatness. His father had educated him carefully in statecraft and early allowed him to share his rule. Burgundy was not a fixed part of the empire; the imperial power had become a reality in Italy; Bavaria, Swabia, and Carinthia were held by the crown; Saxony, if perennially disloyal, remained quiescently so; Lorraine and the kingdom of Hungary were peaceful. After two campaigns Henry forced the duke of Bohemia to recognize his suzerainty, and when the Hungarians overthrew their king, Henry restored his new ally to his throne. In 1043 the realm seemed at peace. It was in that year that Henry proclaimed the "Day of Indulgence," in which he renounced all ideas of vengeance on anyone, and urged Germans great and small to do likewise.

Henry was devoted to the Church, but detested its corruption. There was much to detest. In the tenth and eleventh centuries shadowy popes appeared and vanished, were captured or even murdered, as one Italian faction triumphed over the other. The papacy had become profligate, debauched, above all ineffective. Bishops remained independent lords. Usurpation and corruption were taken for granted. Simony had become the rule and the sale of church offices an accepted form of royal revenue. Yet within the Church a reform movement was growing, finding its most significant early expression in monasticism.

When Henry III became king, the degraded Benedict IX had occupied the Chair of Saint Peter for six years. A nephew of John XIX, Benedict was the last of the dynastic popes. He is said to have been only twelve years old at his election, and his open depravity soon became too much even for the Romans, several of whom attempted to assassinate him on the altar. Finally he was driven out of the city, and the bishop of Sabina was elected in his place as Sylvester III. Benedict's supporters rallied together to expel Sylvester, but the boy pope had become tired of Vatican trumpery and is said to have sold the papacy for cash to his godfather, who took the title of Gregory VI.

In spite of the taint of his election, Gregory was a reformist, closely associated with the dynamic Benedictine monk Hildebrand who became his secretary. Nevertheless, when Henry came to Italy in 1046 he deposed Gregory and, brushing aside any lingering claims of the antipopes Benedict and Sylvester, placed the bishop of Bamberg on the papal throne. Clement II, as he was henceforth known, then crowned Henry emperor. His was a worthy but brief papacy under the emperor's shadow, and when he died it was rumored that he had been poisoned by adherents of Benedict IX. Henry's second appointed pope lived only twenty-three days, dying of either malaria or poison. Then Henry through the transparency of still another election chose his close relative, Bishop Bruno of Toul, to become Leo IX. It was a fateful choice that would change both the papacy and the empire. For in Leo the reformist movement found a pope who would breathe a new spirit into the Church, who would bring leadership and power to the papacy.

Henry's last years were troubled by incursions of the Slavs beyond the Elbe and the Oder, by restiveness in the west culminating in a revolt by Godfrey the Bearded, duke of Upper Lorraine, by a breaking away of Hungary, and by simmering discontent in semi-independent Saxony. At his death in 1056 the emperor seemed weary of life, dubious of the Germany he had built up and that was indeed not to stand. The papal power that he had nurtured would grow until it would destroy his son.

Henry IV was only three when the princes elected him king and swore to accept him as Henry III's successor. Three years later his father died. His mother Agnes became regent, a woman noted more for her piety than her intelligence. Most of the misfortunes of Henry's reign stem from the misrule of the regency. The leading nobles used Agnes' weakness to build up their own power. Godfrey of Lorraine completely usurped the royal authority in Italy. The papacy waxed independent. Saxon lords, always intractable, boldly encroached on the royal domain. After Agnes had been regent for six years, the young king was kidnapped by the powerful and devious Anno, archbishop of Cologne. Anno allied himself with the Saxon nobles and assumed the regency. Though Anno was later ousted by his enemy, Archbishop Adalbert of Bremen, Henry remained a helpless ward until at sixteen he became of age and, ill-prepared though he was, assumed the kingship in his own right.

Henry was intelligent but undisciplined, resolute but impetuous. His reign was a series of ups and downs that ended in disaster and betrayal. At first, with the prestige of the monarchy still intact, he seemed on the way to recovering what had been lost in his minority. When the Saxon nobles revolted against his attempts to garrison and fortify that region in 1075, he yielded temporarily, but later with the aid of the dukes of Swabia, Bavaria, and Carinthia, he was able to bring the Saxons to terms. With Germany at last ostensibly at peace,

he turned to his Italian kingdom where the reinvigorated papacy had steadily been absorbing the imperial prerogatives.

Leo IX had held annual councils, had carefully surrounded himself with reformist cardinals, centralized the authority of the papacy, and in his four-year reign begun to refound papal power. During the minority of Henry IV the imperial nomination of the popes had lapsed. Five popes followed Leo, their names scarcely remembered, until in 1073 Hildebrand was elected as Gregory VII. A small, ugly man with flashing eyes, vigorous and insistent, he would become one of the great popes of history, creator of the centralized papal monarchy. For him the power of the papacy was the power of God. He saw himself as the successor to Saint Peter, the vicar to whom Christ had given the very keys to the kingdom of Heaven. Even as that kingdom surpassed all earthly kingdoms, so should the papal power take precedence over all earthly power, even that of emperors. Rulers were liable to papal judgment, but the pope could be judged by no man.

Henry IV wanted no friendship with the papacy that would subordinate his empire. When at the Lenten synod of 1073 Pope Alexander II had excommunicated five of Henry's councilors, the king refused to dis-

The gilded copper burial crown of Henry IV, who was interred in an unconsecrated grave as the result of his unsuccessful challenge to papal authority

miss them and was himself consequently placed under ban. Gregory on his accession attempted a reconciliation with Henry, who, fearful of his precarious situation in Saxony where the nobles had actually put him to flight, proffered the pope his loyalty and obedience. But with his victory in Saxony in 1075 and his imprisonment of the nobles who had there opposed him, Henry felt free to move against the claims of the papacy. Gregory, in demanding that Henry give up the institution of investiture, had struck at the very basis of Salian powers, for the selling of church offices was a major source of revenue to the crown. Henry's investiture of the archbishop of Milan, granting him authority to make appointments to the sees of Fermo and Spoleto, was a direct challenge to Gregory, who privately threatened him with excommunication. Henry replied haughtily to Hildebrand, "at present not pope but false monk," that he had received his kingdom from God and could be deposed only for apostasy. He then summoned a council of German bishops at Worms, where two archbishops and twenty-four bishops renounced their allegiance to the pope, a step followed shortly by a council of northern Italian bishops. Gregory's response was to depose the bishops, deprive Henry of his German and Italian thrones, absolve his subjects from their oaths of allegiance, and excommunicate Henry.

In challenging Gregory, Henry had overestimated his own strength. Fearful of the king's unrestricted power, the dukes of Swabia, Bavaria, and Carinthia took advantage of the excommunication to come out against him, as did the Saxon leaders who had managed to escape the guard Henry had set over them. The bishops who had sat in condemnation at Worms now hastened to make peace with the pope. Henry was helpless. A diet of nobles decreed that he must obtain absolution within a year or lose his kingdom, and they invited Gregory to Augsburg to decide on Henry's fitness to reign. The only way of avoiding such a conjunction of his lay and clerical enemies, Henry felt, was in a flight across the Alps and a personal appeal to Pope Gregory. With his wife and infant son, Henry crossed into Italy in January, 1073, by way of the formidable Mont Cenis pass. Then, after making his way to Canossa, the castle-fortress belonging to Countess Matilda of Tuscany, he stood in the castle's snow-packed courtyard. "For three days continuously, laying aside all royal pomp, in wretched guise, barefoot and clad in humble woolens," he cast himself on Gregory's mercy.

Even Gregory's stoutest supporters now took pity on the royal penitent. That Gregory kept Henry waiting for three days was not a matter of pride, however, but of genuine perplexity as to how to deal trustworthily with an untrustworthy man. Finally the pope absolved the penitent, receiving him back into the Church after reiterated promises of obedience. Gregory's unexpected action dismayed the German nobles, who had resolved to rid themselves of Henry. Meeting in a diet at Forchheim under the presidency of the archbishop of Mainz, they deposed Henry and elected Duke Rudolf of Swabia king.

For the next three years Germany was subjected to an indecisive civil war, more a matter of skirmishes than battles. Rudolf with the Saxon army had the better soldiers, Henry the greater numbers. But Henry was far more adroit politically in subverting Rudolf's supporters. Gregory now claimed that it was for him to decide which of the two should be king. Henry first appealed to the pope, then threatened him. In reply at a Lenten synod in 1080, Gregory gave his decision in favor of Rudolf, depriving Henry of his kingdom and again excommunicating him.

Now it was Gregory's turn to see his position undermined and his hopes shattered. Henry's party having steadily gained strength in Germany, he called a council of German nobles and bishops on three separate occasions in three different cities, decreed the deposition of the pope, and in 1080 nominated the archbishop of Ravenna as his successor. Certain that his cause would be judged just by God, Gregory predicted that the impious Henry would either be dead or deposed in a few months. Instead, it was Rudolf who died, while Henry moved with an army to Italy.

In desperation the pope turned to the Norman Robert Guiscard, duke of Apulia, Calabria, and Sicily, who had himself recently been under the papal ban. Guiscard, occupied with a revolt in the south of Italy, did not act until the following year. During that time Henry crossed the Alps, and after an initial repulse, captured Rome and Saint Peter's and placed his own nominee on the papal throne as Clement III. Gregory took refuge in the Castle of Sant'Angelo. Clement III was enthroned, and one of his first acts was to crown Henry emperor.

For two years Clement III seemed master of Rome, recognized through most of Germany and northern Italy. But his support dwindled, his position gradually eroded, until in the end he too found himself isolated and abandoned in Sant'Angelo Castle. After Victor III's interlude reign, Urban II became pope; an ardent follower of Gregory, with deft persistence he expanded his power even into heretofore imperial Lombardy.

So serious did the situation in northern Italy appear to Henry that he felt impelled to journey there in force. In 1087 he had obtained the election and coronation of his eldest son Conrad, and two years after—following the death of his wife—he married the Russian princess Praxedis. A few years later, in the midst of an Italian campaign which was at first successful, he found himself faced by a revolt of his own son who had come to Italy and joined the papal party, doing fealty to Urban and receiving in return both the Iron Crown of Lombardy and the promise of the imperial crown. Praxedis too deserted her husband, joining the enemy to accuse him of all manner of vice and cruelty. Overwhelmed by his treacherous coalition, opposed by a league of Lombard cities, Henry could make no headway against his Italian enemies.

In 1097 he returned to Germany with his authority much impaired, even though the country itself was at peace. Still excommunicated, his Italian kingdom lost, he found himself dependent now on the sufferance of his nobles with whom he now made his peace. They in turn agreed to recognize his second son Henry as heir to the crown. But his southern duchies had become almost as independent as Saxony.

Henry the son had sworn never to act with independent authority during his father's lifetime. But increasingly conscious of the emperor's weakened position, he finally and suddenly came out in revolt, allying himself with the papal party in Germany, and the discontented lesser nobles. Other princes, like the duke of Bavaria, remained neutral in the struggle, and Henry IV lacked the strength to bring his son to heel. Young Henry finally persuaded his father to an interview, then treacherously made him prisoner. The following year, 1106, the emperor managed to escape and, with the support of Lorraine and the emerging Rhineland cities, twice defeated his son's forces. But that August before any really decisive encounter, the elder Henry died. For five years his body lay in an unconsecrated grave.

Henry IV had failed to re-establish royal control over the papacy, whose authority over the bishops would, thanks to Gregory, not again be in dispute. More significant than this, Henry had failed to overcome the autonomy of the German nobles, a failure that would echo through centuries of German history.

The year before his father's death, Henry V had taken care to make peace with the Church. But the peace would be a short one, for his nineteen-year reign would be marked by a great investiture struggle. Pope Gregory's decree of 1075 had forbidden lay investiture—the royal bestowal of the ring and staff which were the outward symbols of a bishop's office. The new pope, Paschal II, expecting immediate compliance with papal decrees, found that Henry V had no intention of giving up what had long been the royal right. Though Paschal refused to compromise on the investiture, Henry was politic enough at first not to challenge him directly, not at least until Paschal had crowned him emperor, as the pope now agreed to do.

Henry marched with a large army to Rome for his coronation in 1111 and on the way was able to restore his authority over the Italian kingdom. Even the Normans were this time overawed by the size of the imperial army. In Rome, Henry's bodyguard surrounded the pope and cardinals, and Paschal was held a prisoner until he conceded to Henry the right of investiture and agreed to crown him emperor. The humiliation of the pope, it turned out, gained Henry little, for when he returned to Germany, Paschal repudiated what had been extorted from him. Henry's last decade was further troubled by revolts. Nor did he have the force to act finally against the revived independence of the duchies. When the old ducal line died out in troublesome Saxony, he appointed Lothair of Supplinburg to the dukedom, only to find that Lothair's sole concern was to create a strong independent duchy for himself. Swabia alone, with Henry's trustworthy nephew Frederick the One-Eyed installed as its duke, remained unwaveringly loyal to him.

In 1113 Siegfried, count palatine of the Rhine, launched a revolt against the king in which he was joined by the Saxon nobles and Henry's own chancellor, Archbishop Adalbert of Mainz. Henry, nevertheless, decisively defeated them. Adalbert was made prisoner, and Siegfried died of battle wounds. The following January Henry married Matilda, daughter of Henry I of England. Not long after, revolt again broke out, first in Cologne, then spreading through Lorraine. The Saxons under Duke Lothair joined the rebels, and the papal legates in

Saxony pronounced Henry excommunicate. More carefully organized this time, the rebel leaders twice defeated Henry on the battlefield and forced him to release Adalbert, who proceeded to Cologne. There Adalbert in defiance excommunicated the king.

Henry had by now lost control of the northern part of his kingdom, but the fighting did not spread to the south and it soon became desultory. When in 1115 Matilda of Tuscany died, leaving her possessions to her "cousin" Henry V, the emperor again set out for Italy, undoubtedly expecting when there to deal once more with the question of investiture. But Paschal, at the news of his coming, fled to the Normans in the south. Henry and the English Matilda were crowned by the archbishop of Braga, who was promptly excommunicated by the absent Paschal. After the coronation, Henry set up the compliant archbishop as Pope Gregory VIII, while Gelasius II, who had just succeeded Paschal, excommunicated both antipope and emperor. Gelasius lived only a year. The next pope, Calixtus II, renewed the excommunication.

On returning to Germany Henry found that Archbishop Adalbert had aligned most of the bishops against him, but the lay nobles showed themselves less eager to embrace the papal cause or renew an indeterminate civil war. The duke of Swabia and Henry the Black, soon to become duke of Bavaria, took the lead in calling a diet at Wurzburg to end domestic dissension and bring peace between pope and emperor, though it is a sign of the emperor's weakness that it was left to the nobles to make the peace. Pope Calixtus compliantly sent three cardinals as his emissaries. The settlement that was reached in 1122 became known as the Concordat of Worms. In it Henry renounced investiture with ring and staff and guaranteed free canonical elections in Italy and the security of ecclesiastical possessions. He in turn was received back into the Church, and was allowed to invest church funds and to control appointments in Germany. Calixtus confirmed the settlement in the Lateran basilica in a council which, ending the schism between pope and emperor, came to be known as the First Lateran Council.

In 1125 the childless Henry died. On his deathbed he tried to assure the continuity of his house by having his nephew, Duke Frederick of Swabia, succeed him. But Adalbert, who as archbishop of Mainz would play a leading part in any new election, was implacably opposed. There would be no Salian successor.

506

CHAPTER V

ERA OF HOHENSTAUFEN STABILITY

Otto the Great had brought stability and security to his realm after a long period of chaos. In the tenth and eleventh centuries the population grew. Woods rang with axes as forests gave way to fields, and everywhere building went on. Most notable was the construction of churches and monasteries, in the style that would be known as Romanesque, and architects and sculptors evolved new concepts as they reshaped traditional patterns. Cathedrals and churches still had flat, timbered ceilings, but at Speyer about 1090 Henry IV built the first stone-vaulted nave in Europe (though it later collapsed). With security came the revival of trade and commerce and, as a concomitant, the rebirth of the towns and the emergence of a new class, the merchant, the burgher.

Most towns like Strasbourg or Mainz had begun as a fort by a river, a garrison center; then, after the collapse of Roman rule and their reduction to skeletons, they underwent a slow refleshing through lay and clerical overlordship to a self-governing community rich and powerful enough to resist all assailants. Those towns, their formidably constructed walls sheltering crafts and guilds and trades and manu-

An architect, holding one of the drafting tools of his profession, by Dürer

factures, became islands of safety and wealth, drawing in the vigorous and the enterprising from the countryside. By revolt or purchase, or both, the cities came to achieve their charters of independence from their lords.

The growth of the cities was accelerated by the crusades. In Gibbons' measured words, "the estates of the barons were dissipated and their race often extinguished in these costly and perilous expeditions. Their poverty extorted from their pride those charters of freedom which unlocked the fetters of the slave, secured the farm of the peasant, and the shop of the artificer, and gradually restored a substance and soul to the most useful part of the community."

Henry IV—still excommunicate—and the German princes had not participated in the First Crusade, proclaimed by Urban II at Clermont in 1095. But the Frenchman Peter the Hermit, aflame with fanatic zeal and leading his inappropriately named Peasants' Crusade to the Holy Land, drew after him the young, the restless, the drifters. Their zeal often found its outlet in plunder and looting and in attacks on the wealthy and hitherto undisturbed Jewish congregations, the "unbelievers." Some would eventually reach Syria. Few if any would return.

By the time the Salian line came to an end in 1125, the Crusaders had been in possession of captured Jerualem for a quarter of a century and the kingdom of Jerusalem had been established there. Henry V's dying wish to have his nephew Frederick the One-Eyed of Swabia, head of the house of Hohenstaufen, succeed him was nullified by the church party led by his old enemy Archbishop Adalbert. The hereditary principle that the Saxon and Salian rulers had striven for was thereby discarded in favor of the more ancient principle of tribal election. Ten representatives each from Bavaria, Swabia, Franconia, and Saxony were chosen for a rudimentary assembly that would evolve in time into the electoral college of princes. Following Adalbert's skilled maneuvering, Lothair, duke of Saxony and a constant opponent of the Salian dynasty, was chosen over Duke Frederick.

Lothair II, son of a petty count, could not trace his pedigree beyond his own father, but by marriage to the Welf heiress of the counts of Nordheim and Brunswick he had acquired so dominant a position in Saxony that he finally succeeded the ruling Duke Magnus, who died without heirs. Four families, the Welfs and the Hohenstaufens (known more lastingly by their Italian designations as the Guelphs and the Ghibellines), the Wettins and the Wittelsbachs, were emerging to replace the old nobility that had become extinct in the wars. Henry IV had founded the fortunes of both the Welfs and the Hohenstaufens, the former when he gave the duchy of Bavaria to Welf IV, and the latter when he made Frederick I of Staufen duke of Swabia and granted him his daughter Agnes in marriage.

Lothair's election was followed by widespread unrest and resistance on the part of the Hohenstaufens. Most of his reign would indeed be shadowed by the Welf-Hohenstaufen feud. When Frederick the One-Eyed refused to yield fiefs claimed by Lothair and was found guilty of treason, a clash between the elderly king and the highhanded young duke was inevitable. At first Lothair hesitated, but after the marriage of his daughter Gertrude to the new Welf duke of Bavaria, Henry the Proud, he felt strong enough to launch a punitive expedition against his challenger. His first efforts, when he attempted to capture the Hohenstaufen stronghold of Nuremberg, broke down as Frederick's younger brother Conrad, returning from the Crusade, countermarched his troops and broke the siege. Conrad's supporters now elected him king with his brother's acquiescence. But the church hierarchy that had placed Lothair on the throne threw their support to him. Unable to cope with the military might of the bishops, Conrad fled to Italy, where although he was crowned in Milan with the Iron Crown of Lombardy, his further efforts came to nothing. Lothair's son-in-law, Duke Henry, managed to contain Frederick the One-Eyed in the south. But the struggle was unending. The sequence of revolts, battles, sieges, and confiscations tore Germany apart. Frederick and Conrad, their castles taken, their supporters drifting away, finally made their submission to Lothair, who generously restored to them their confiscated possessions. Before this truce with the house of Hohenstaufen, Lothair had intervened in the disputed papal election following the death of Honorius II when two rivals, Anacletus II in Rome and Innocent II in France, proclaimed themselves pope. Taking the side of Innocent, Lothair marched on Rome, installed his candidate, and as a reward was crowned emperor. A year after the submission of the Hohenstaufens, Lothair again crossed the Alps to campaign against Roger of Sicily but died of a sudden illness in a peasant's hut on the way back.

Lothair had made the natural and obvious choice of his son-in-law, Henry the Proud, as his successor by leaving him the duchies of Bavaria, Swabia, and Saxony and entrusting him with the imperial insignia. Yet the Church and lay princes who had elected Lothair feared the might of his Welf son-in-law, the most powerful and wealthy prince in Germany, and feared even more the revival of the hereditary principle. Taking the lead, the archbishop of Trier, who had long been at odds with Henry, summoned an assembly that chose Conrad of Hohenstaufen emperor. Ten days later Conrad was crowned at Aachen by the papal legate.

At first Conrad III was a popular choice. Young, energetic, and personable, he seemed an acceptable counterweight to the power of the Welfs. Even Henry the Proud was willing to accept the inevitable, delivering up the royal insignia with the understanding that he would be confirmed in his two dukedoms. Conrad, however, had already promised Saxony to that rival of the Welfs, Albert the Bear of Brandenburg. Henry, on learning this, threatened revolt. Conrad countered by placing him under the ban of empire and making Albert duke. Shortly afterward, he gave Bavaria to his half brother, Leopold of Austria.

Henry the Proud was as good as his threat. Before Conrad's coronation year was out, Saxony and Bavaria blazed with civil war. The banished Henry reappeared in Saxony and the people and prince of that stubbornly independent duchy rallied to him. Albert was driven out. Conrad, undaunted, assembled a punitive expedition that included the archbishops of Mainz and Trier, the bishops of Worms and Speyer, and the new rulers of Saxony and Bavaria. But the armies of Conrad and Henry, when they at last confronted each other, showed little lust for combat. A conference was held in which conviviality, aided by thirty tuns of wine, overcame hostility. Then the two armies, after pledging their mutual health with the last of the wine, separated with swords sheathed, leaving Henry the master of Saxony and Conrad's candidate, Duke Albert, deserted by the few Saxon nobles who had sided with him.

In Bavaria Conrad's cause fared better: Leopold was easily accepted by his new subjects, who distrusted the short-tempered Henry. Meanwhile, Henry was making plans to recover Bavaria by force of arms when he died in 1139 in his thirtieth year, so suddenly and unaccountably that the rumor spread that he had been poisoned. His death was a great blow to the Welf cause, as his heir—later to be known as Henry the Lion—was a mere boy of ten. Albert's way back to Saxony seemed open. Unfortunately for him, his attempt to conquer the stubborn duchy ended in complete failure. Welf fortunes took a turn for the better when Welf VI, Henry the Proud's brother, rallied to the family cause and attacked and defeated Leopold. The turn of fortune was only temporary. Conrad and his brother Frederick, hastening south with their forces, shattered Welf's army, then besieged and finally captured the Welfic fortress of Weinsberg. According to legend the men of Weinsberg were condemned to death, while the women were spared and allowed to leave, taking with them what they could carry away on their backs. They chose to carry their men!

Conrad's imposing victory not only crushed the rebellion but it gave second thoughts to many of the Saxon princes. The king was ready for a compromise and summoned a diet at Frankfurt. Since Leopold had died, Conrad for a time kept the duchy of Austria in his own hands, then awarded it to Leopold's brother, Henry Jasomirgott (so nicknamed after his favorite oath). Henry the Lion was left in possession of Saxony, and Albert the Bear was induced to renounce his title in exchange for territory in the north that he had previously held. Then Conrad issued a general pardon to all who had taken part in the rebellion, and as a token of reconciliation married off Henry the Proud's widow to Jasomirgott.

The settlement that appeared so fair was fleeting. As a chronicler of the time observed, "it was the seed of the greatest disaster in our land." Frederick the One-Eyed, enraged by the award of Bavaria to his half brother Jasomirgott, for a time made overtures to the Welfs, who still refused to accept the loss of Bavaria. Never again would he be on terms of intimacy and friendship with his brother. The last thread binding the settlement snapped when Jasomirgott's wife Gertrude died in childbirth.

Much of Conrad's troubles stemmed from his attempts to provide for his overabundant relatives. His mother Agnes, after the death of Frederick I of Staufen, had married Leopold III of Austria and by her two marriages bore twenty-three children, all claimants of their blood privilege. Conrad's grant of the duchy of Lower Lorraine to one brother-in-law led to a rising in that region; the marriage of two half sisters to the claimants to the dukedom of Poland and the dukedom of Bohemia involved him in strife in both these countries. Then, to add to his difficulties, the year 1146 brought a devastating famine across the land.

The Second Crusade, preached by Bernard of Clairvaux, to relieve the once-more-threatened Holy Places did much to ease the inner tension in Germany, even though the Crusade itself was a disaster. Welf VI and Henry Jasomirgott were among the nobles who took the cross, and Conrad, after hearing Bernard preach at Christmas in the Cathedral of Speyer, made his own vow in spite of the uncertain conditions of his realm. In the spring of 1147, after overseeing the election and coronation of his ten-year-old son, Henry, as king, Conrad left for the Holy Land. By special dispensation, the pope allowed some of the Saxons, including Duke Henry the Lion, and Albert the Bear, to make their crusade against the heathen Wends who had been encroaching from the east.

Both ventures ended futilely. The Wendish Crusade bogged down in selfish recriminations among the leaders. Conrad with his contingent reached the Holy Land only to suffer a crushing defeat at Dorylaeum. A year later he took part in the siege of Damascus. Finding his efforts vitiated by the jealousies of the French contingent, he abandoned the siege and returned home in disgust.

Before Conrad had left on the Crusade, Henry the Lion, repudiating the settlement made by his guardians, presented his demands for the dukedom of Bavaria. Conrad managed to put him off until his return, but with the king back in Germany, Henry renewed his claim, and when he received no response assumed on his own the title of duke of Bavaria and Saxony. His was a formidable challenge. Henry, for all his youth, had increased his strength and support, while Conrad's position had weakened. The rest of Conrad's reign was marked by inconclusive campaigns, truces, negotiations, the calling of imperial diets, and increasing distress in a dispirited land exhausted by the ravaging passages of armed men. Conrad made every effort to undermine Duke Henry's position in Saxony, doing his best to suborn the duke's supporters while making secret plans to seize his capital at Brunswick. But Conrad's efforts came to nothing, and finally he abandoned Saxony altogether.

Frederick Barbarossa with Otto von Freising, historian and bishop of the twelfth-century cathedral of Freising, where this carving appears

FREDERIC ROM
IMPR AVGVST

He died a short while later in February, 1152. He had been an unlikely king. At the beginning of his reign most of his subjects had welcomed him. He was brave, pious, and energetic. He had avoided controversies with the Church. Yet he was incapable of dealing with the Welf-Hohenstaufen feud that was rending Germany, and he left his kingdom in an almost complete state of disintegration.

Young King Henry had died before his father, and Conrad on his deathbed knew that there was little chance for his next son, the six-year-old Frederick, to succeed him. With this realization he designated his nephew Frederick of Swabia as his successor and entrusted the royal insignia to him. Frederick, now the head of the house of Hohenstaufen, was equally bound to both Hohenstaufen and Welf, for his father was Frederick the One-Eyed, brother of the late King Conrad, while his mother was the sister of Henry the Proud. The princes who gathered in the diet at Frankfurt to elect him were unanimous in their choice. Not in generations had a king been so welcomed.

The new king and emperor—for upon his election he became automatically Holy Roman Emperor, although he would not be crowned for another three years—was thirty years old, of more than middle height, singularly handsome, vigorous in mind and body, with a face always ready to break out in a smile. A man who loved hunting, riding, and swimming, a courageous fighter who exulted in combat, he seemed the very embodiment of medieval chivalry. His most striking physical characteristic was his red beard, for which he would go down in history as Barbarossa; in generations to come he would be as legendary a figure as Charlemagne, whom he so much resembled. For he had his great predecessor's energy, decisiveness, judgment, and qualities of leadership. Though not a scholar, he admired scholarship. Though he could not speak Latin, he understood it. In his own tongue he was eloquent. He was interested in history and in his ancestral past. A friend of Roman lawyers, he became a great lawgiver. Deeply pious, he led a blameless life. Better than anyone else he came to express the imperial ideal.

In his reign of almost forty years he revived the "grandeur of the empire in all its former glory." He had come to a Germany internally riven by conflict between Welf and Hohenstaufen, externally subservient to papal power. Feudalism in Italy had whittled away the imperial authority to almost nothing. In Germany he proceeded to restore the power and prestige of the monarchy by reclaiming the loyalty of the princes of the crown. In Italy, he enforced his authority as emperor over both nobles and independent cities while reducing the influence and authority of the pope. He called a diet and imposed the election of his four-year-old son Henry VI as coemperor with the revived title of caesar and saw him finally ruler of Sicily. Not since Charlemagne and Otto the Great had any emperor been so successful, so admired, and honored.

Shortly after Frederick's election he informed various notables that he intended to re-establish the honor and strength of the kingdom and the empire, and that if he failed he would consider his honor lost. His Holy Roman Empire embraced the kingdoms of Germany, Burgundy, and Italy. Burgundy was subsidiary. Germany would be pacified and controlled. The key to the empire was in Italy. Shortly after his coronation he issued a royal proclamation regulating the peace of his realm and ordering his princes to cease their feuds. He gained their initial cooperation by recognizing their natural rights and appealing to their sense of honor, while at the same time showing that he was not prepared to relinquish any of his crown rights. He also made it clear that although he approved of the effort of the Council of Worms to define the limits of temporal and spiritual authority, he intended to maintain firm control of all episcopal nominations.

Frederick preferred cooperation to compulsion and this he found possible in Germany. Italy was another matter, and wherever he was opposed there he replied with brute force. He wished to have harmonious relations with the papacy, but with the understanding that he must have control over general policy in Italy with the Holy See restricting itself to questions of ecclesiastical administration. The problem of Italy would occupy him for the next twenty years, would force him to install his own candidates on the papal throne, and involve him in six campaigns there, one of which would bring about his defeat by the combined forces of the Italian cities of the Lombard League.

In 1154 he set off on his first expedition to Italy with a relatively small force, as the German princes had been reluctant to participate. On the way he learned of the death of the pope, Anastasius IV. Anastasius was succeeded by the English cardinal Nicholas Breakspear, who as Adrian IV would soon find that his authority did not extend beyond the walls of the Vatican. Rome itself was in the hands of the merchants and the old aristocracy who had proclaimed a commune under the passionately reformist monk Arnold of Brescia. Though Adrian viewed Frederick with some suspicion, the latter made the conciliatory gesture of capturing Arnold and turning him over to the clerical authorities for execution. With the German army occupying Rome, Frederick attended high mass at Saint Peter's, and after the Epistle had been read, Adrian handed him the imperial sword and sceptre and finally the golden crown. Frederick was now Holy Roman Emperor. Although many of the northern cities, headed by Milan, still refused to accept his authority, he felt he could no longer keep his small and now plague-ridden army in Italy; after enjoining the Romans to remain faithful to the pope, he returned to Germany.

The three years that he now spent in his native country were a time of consolidation and of planning a more extensive expedition to bring Italy's northern cities to heel. He pacified Henry the Lion with the duchy of Bavaria while appeasing Henry Jasomirgott by raising the East March (Austria) to an independent duchy. Having with papal permission divorced his barren wife, he now consolidated his position still further by marrying Beatrice, the heiress of the count of Burgundy. He established friendly relations with the duke of Bohemia and the king of Hungary while launching a brief punitive campaign into Poland. North of the Alps peace and order reigned in his empire.

Meanwhile, Pope Adrian, increasingly uneasy at Frederick's growing power, had signed the Concordat of Benevento with his erstwhile enemy King William of Sicily. Frederick, who had counted on papal support against William's kingdom, was outraged. He now called up a huge German army, with allied contingents from Bohemia, Hungary, and Poland, and led his forces across the Alps.

His goal was to bring Lombardy under his control, then Tuscany, the Papal States, and Rome in preparation for a final attack upon Sicily. After a month's siege he forced Milan to submit but treated the conquered city leniently in the hope that the Milanese example would persuade the other cities to do the same. Frederick's massive Italian intervention so alarmed the pope that he was preparing to excommunicate the emperor. Then in 1159 Adrian died.

Barbarossa was destined to spend the next six years in Italy. Time and again his goal of uniting the country under his imperial rule seemed almost within his grasp, only to elude him. Adrian's death he took as an opportunity to name the pro-German Cardinal Octavian as pope. When the Sacred College rejected Frederick's candidate, Octavian's armed supporters broke up the assemblage and installed him as Victor IV. The majority of cardinals then elected the anti-German Alexander III, an astute, gifted priest-politician who saw himself as the champion of the Church's liberties and who proceeded at once to excommunicate Frederick, whom he branded as "the chief persecutor of the Church of God."

Frederick was never able to get the support he had hoped for Victor IV nor for the succeeding antipopes, Paschal III and Calixtus III. Depleted in his forces, unable to crush the resistance in the Lombard cities, Frederick retired to Germany. There at a diet assembled at Aachen during Christmas, 1165, he had Charlemagne's body exhumed and placed where it could be more easily venerated. Asserting the authority of Paschal III, the emperor proclaimed the canonization of his great predecessor.

While Frederick was in Germany, Pope Alexander, with Sicilian support, returned to Rome and even engineered a *rapprochement* between Sicily and the Byzantine emperor. Frederick determined now to raise another army and march straight on Rome. He crossed the Brenner in the autumn of 1166, wintered in Lodi where he was joined by allied contingents, and, as soon as the weather lightened, thrust for Rome, driving out the papal defenders and placing Paschal III on the Chair of Saint Peter. Paschal again crowned Frederick and he in turn declared that Rome was now his capital. Emperor in the Eternal City, he seemed indeed the fated successor of the caesars. Then fate struck him down. Shortly after his coronation in August, 1167, torrential storms flooded Rome. The sewers overflowed, and in the fetid heat that followed, pestilence swept through the German army, forcing Barbarossa to lead the dispirited remnants of his soldiery to the cleaner air of upper Italy. Most of the Lombard cities, sixteen of them headed by Venice and the reconstituted Milan, seized the occasion to turn against him, banding together to form the Lombard League. The emperor now found himself without support. Within weeks his work of

a decade had fallen apart, and he had to slip away from Italy in disguise. The peninsula seemed lost to him for good.

The next six years Frederick Barbarossa remained in Germany. Not only did his northern kingdom demand his attention, not only did he lack the resources for a renewed Italian campaign, but beyond those factors lay his growing awareness that the velvet glove of diplomacy could be as effective as the mailed fist. When Alexander formed an alliance with the Lombard League, Frederick's first response was to try to divert him. The emperor was now willing to recognize Alexander as pope and to make further concessions if Alexander would abandon his urban allies. The pope temporized, then refused. Barbarossa began long-range plans for another military campaign to bring down the Lombard League.

In September, 1174, the emperor crossed the Alps for the fifth time, his small army being made up chiefly of Brabant mercenaries. The Lombard League, with the wealth of Venice behind it, assembled an army that effectively checked him, the more because he soon found himself running out of money to pay his mercenaries. A temporary truce followed in which (to Frederick's financial relief) both sides agreed to disband their armies. The adversaries failed, however, to agree further, and Frederick decided that the war must go on. Left with only a skeletal force, he received some reinforcements from his Italian allies, but when he appealed for further support to Henry the Lion, that prince called the "haughtiest of mankind" refused. The depleted imperial army met that of the League at Legnano in a battle that became a rout for Frederick after the Lombard infantry broke the German ranks. Even the emperor's personal standard was captured, and for a time he himself was believed to have been killed.

Yet Frederick, routed in battle, did not neglect the lessons of diplomacy. Since his negotiations with the League had always broken down over the recognition of Alexander, he now decided to come to his own terms with the pope. Their haggling resulted in the Peace of Venice, in which Frederick agreed to recognize Alexander, and Alexander agreed to revoke Frederick's excommunication and to recognize him as emperor. Frederick also agreed to a six-year truce with the Lombard cities and to a separate peace with Sicily which he reinforced later by arranging the marriage of his son Henry to the convent-

Episodes of courtly love in a fourteenth-century manuscript: tying the knot; gaining entrance to the castle; walking in the woods; repairing armour

immured Constance, heiress to the Sicilian king William II. Calixtus he disposed of by retiring him to a monastery. The settlement with the pope shook the unity of the Lombard League, and Frederick was now able to come to terms with the individual cities. When he left Italy in 1178, he at last found his imperial position recognized by all.

He had not, however, forgotten his moment of need. On arriving in Germany he accused Henry the Lion of treason and declared all his duchies and fiefs forfeit. When Henry took to arms in protest, he found that most of his vassals had deserted him. After Frederick had captured Brunswick, the duke had no alternative but to sue for pardon. This defeat of the emperor's strongest, most independent prince consolidated and extended Frederick's power still further. At Mainz "the Golden" in 1184 he held a pageant of unexampled splendor in which his two sons were knighted and to which knights and nobles thronged from all over Europe. This pageant of chivalry was itself another step toward Frederick's goal of a hereditary monarchy. Pope Alexander had died in 1181 and was succeeded by Lucius III. The new pope and the emperor met at Verona and agreed to prepare a Third Crusade to safeguard the imperiled Holy Places. But Lucius refused Frederick's request to have his son Henry crowned coemperor, remarking dryly that one emperor was enough.

Not until three popes had succeeded Lucius did the Crusade become an actuality. In 1188, a year after his election to the Chair of Saint Peter, Clement III at last issued the call. In contrast to his immediate predecessors, Clement was a conciliatory churchman, anxious to show himself a loyal ally of the emperor. At the Diet of Christ, Frederick had let it be known that he had taken the cross. He seemed now the very leader of all Christendom. As he made ready to leave for the Holy Land, he had reached the goal he had set for himself at his coronation: king of Germany and Italy, and unchallenged Roman Emperor.

Before Frederick could leave on his crusade, the West was stunned by the fall of Jerusalem. Religious zeal as well as the ambition to be the rescuer of the Holy City now urged the emperor forward. In May, 1189, he left Regensburg with some sixty princes and nobles and an army of a hundred thousand—the largest he had ever commanded. Just over a year later, in Little Armenia, he was drowned when his horse shied while crossing the swift waters of the Calycadnus River.

Frederick Barbarossa the legend would engulf the man. As emperor he was in fact the most illustrious of Germany's medieval rulers. Never had the empire been so honored and so feared as at his death. Yet he had built his strength in Germany on the foundation of his princes. These princes, more than a hundred in all—dukes, margraves, landgraves, bishops—held their vast fiefs from the crown, but in turn stood between the emperor and his subjects. As long as they remained loyal, the emperor was strong. But their growing independence was the price he had to pay, and his successors would have to pay, for his Italian campaigns.

Out of the frustrations and longings of future generations the myth would form of the great German emperor who had imposed his will on Italy and the pope, and who died leading a German crusade. Later legend would have it that he was not really dead but asleep in a cave in the Thuringian forest "seated between six knights at a table of stone until the day when, at last, he will deliver Germany from slavery and make her leader of the whole world."

On leaving for the Third Crusade—"the German Crusade"—Frederick had turned over control of the empire to his son, who on his father's death became Henry VI. Henry lacked his father's charm and courage and magnanimity. Even his physical appearance was mean. Yet, though his nature was cruel and treacherous, his vision was large and his mind sharp. He was an educated man, "more learned than men of learning." He spoke Latin almost as if it were his native tongue, and his models of emulation were classical: Caesar, Augustus, and above all Alexander the Great.

Meanwhile, Henry the Lion, who had been exiled to England, had taken advantage of Frederick's absence to return to Saxony and raise the standard of revolt, a revolt that young King Henry finally managed to control before his father's death. In 1189 William II of Sicily died childless, leaving King Henry, through his wife's inheritance, heir to that crown. The Sicilian nobles refused to accept the intruder king, and with the permission of Pope Clement III had Count Tancred of Lecce (the bastard of Sicily's greatest king, Roger II) crowned at Palermo.

Troubles were rising in Germany, where hostilities continued in Saxony and elsewhere. When Pope Clement died in 1191, Henry waited only long enough to be crowned Holy Roman Emperor by his successor, Celestine III, then hastened back across the Alps. Meanwhile, Tancred was extending his control in Sicily, encouraged by the pope who now invested him with the kingdom that comprised Sicily and the south of Italy. At the same time Celestine secretly abetted the spreading dissent in Germany, even as Tancred took steps to aid Henry the Lion and the Welfs.

The emperor found still more solid German opposition after he attempted to settle the disputed election of Albert of Brabant as bishop of Liège. When Albert refused to accept the imperial decision against him and appealed to the pope, Henry declared him guilty of high treason. Shortly afterward Albert was murdered by a party of German knights and, rightly or wrongly, Henry was held responsible. Then in December, 1192, Richard the Lion-Hearted returned from the Crusade, was captured by Duke Leopold of Austria who turned his noble prisoner over to the emperor. The murder of Albert and the imprisonment of a Crusader were acts of impiety that set off a widespread insurrection. Many of the German princes considered deposing Henry. But in the captive English king, Henry held enormous bargaining leverage, enough in the end to save his kingdom. By threatening to turn Richard over to England's archenemy, the French king, Henry was able to extort his own terms. Richard was finally released after a huge ransom was paid. In addition, he was forced to repudiate Tancred, guarantee the submission of the Welfs, and finally yield his kingdom to Henry, receiving it back as the emperor's vassal.

With the tide running so swiftly in his favor, Henry now prepared to bring Sicily to submission. As a preliminary gesture of conciliation he married his cousin to the eldest son of the now aged Henry the Lion, and took him in his entourage on the campaign. Luck continued to favor the emperor. Through his diplomacy Sicily had been deprived of the support of Richard and the Welfs. Then Tancred died, leaving a mere boy as heir without any substantial advisers. No strong force was left to oppose Henry's Sicilian advance. His progress through the south of Italy seemed more a march than a campaign, with Salerno the only city offering any resistance. He reached Palermo with the empress Constance and was crowned king on Christmas Day, 1194. The very next day the forty-year-old Constance, after nine childless years, gave birth to the son who would become Frederick II.

Henry now ruled from the North Sea to the southern tip of Italy. England was his vassal kingdom, and France and Spain and Byzantium might fall within his grasp. Before him glittered the vision of world domination such as Alexander had once achieved. With an heir now granted him, he was eager to forge a hereditary dynasty. To bypass the electoral princes he now maneuvered to have his son Frederick baptized and anointed king of the Romans by the pope. Yet to all the emperor's conciliatory gestures, even the offer to undertake a new crusade, Pope Celestine remained aloof, temporizing, even as the German princes rallied to oppose Henry's plan. Henry was preparing his crusade when a revolt broke out in Sicily against the harshness of his rule. This revolt he put down with the utmost cruelty, torturing and even crucifying some of his captured opponents, and blinding those Sicilian nobles who had previously been interned in German prisons. In September, 1197, the main body of Henry's German crusaders embarked for the Holy Land. Before the 33-year-old emperor could follow he came down with a fever brought on by a night of hunting in the woodlands of Linari. He died a few days later and was buried in the Cathedral of Palermo, leaving succeeding generations to speculate what he might have achieved if he had lived as long as his father.

With Henry's death, Hohenstaufen plans for dominion and hereditary rule collapsed. The Italians seized the longed-for opportunity to expel their German officials and German governors. In Germany it was out of the question for the princes to elect the three-year-old Frederick to the uneasy throne. Henry's brother and confidant, Philip of Swabia, would have favored his nephew's candidacy if it had been possible. Since it was not, he himself accepted the proffered crown. A minority of the princes, however, elected Otto of Brunswick; this son of Henry the Lion was backed by his uncle, Richard the Lion-Hearted, who saw in him a means of opposing King Philip Augustus of France. Again the Welf-Hohenstaufen feud blazed up, engulfing Germany in sixteen years of desolation and pillage.

In Sicily, Markward of Anweiler, Henry's lieutenant, announced himself as Frederick's vice-regent. The dowager queen Constance, who had tried to salvage at least her own kingdom by having the child Frederick crowned in Palermo, appealed to Innocent for protection. He, the youngest and as it would prove the greatest of the medieval popes, accepted the guardianship of the boy king after Constance's death. Yet Innocent's protecting arm was not long enough to prevent Markward from kidnapping the boy. In spite of his captivity and in spite of the violence and rapine in his kingdom, Frederick II nevertheless survived to the age of fourteen when he became king of Sicily at last in his own right. The kingdom of Sicily under Frederick's sternly able rule would reach a state of civilization and prosperity higher than any other country in Europe. "Stupor mundi" (the wonder of the world) Frederick would come to be called. As he grew in power he was able to hold Sicily and southern Italy in a dictator's grasp. A sensualist, a poet, a latent freethinker who hated the papacy, with his learning and his cultivated cruelty, his Saracen soldiers and his Byzantine court and menagerie and harem, he seemed rather a Greek ruler than a Western emperor—and so he liked to think himself.

Innocent had taken skillful advantage of the weakness of imperial power to re-establish the power of the papacy, to regain control of Rome itself and of the Patrimony of Saint Peter—the area surrounding the city—as well as most of the Papal States. In the quarrel of the German kings he continued to favor the Welfic Otto of Brunswick, but when Philip of Swabia's triumph seemed certain he changed course and agreed to crown the Hohenstaufen. Before Philip could reach Rome he was murdered for some private grievance by the count palatine of Bavaria, Otto of Wittelsbach. The strife-wearied German princes then turned to Otto of Brunswick, stipulating only that he marry Philip's eleven-year-old daughter Beatrice as a gesture of peace between the two houses.

A fear that haunted the popes was that of having the kingdom of Sicily united to the empire to create a super-state that would reduce the papacy to a dependency. Before agreeing to crown Otto emperor, in 1209, Innocent had insisted that he recognize Sicily as a papal fief. Yet the previously subservient Otto had not been crowned a month before he launched a Sicilian expedition to oust Frederick. Innocent, betrayed, appealed to the bishops and princes of Germany. Otto, well on the way to conquering Sicily, found his position in his own country so endangered that he was forced to hurry back across the Alps. Frederick, too, had left for Germany where he was now offered the crown by dissident princes. Again the forces of Welf and Hohenstaufen confronted each other. Curiously enough the actual test of arms took place in France where Philip Augustus, who had allied himself with Frederick, found himself opposed by the army supplied by King John of England (successor to his brother Richard, John continued to support Otto). The defeat of the Anglo-German army at Bouvines, in which John almost lost his crown, was even more of a defeat for Otto, who was wounded in battle. Frederick, with no forces left to oppose him, was crowned king of Germany at Aachen in 1215.

The end result of the civil war was to weaken fatally the German kingdom as well as the Holy Roman Empire. For Philip, Otto and Frederick, in seeking the support of the nobles and the towns, had outbid one another in bartering away lands and prerogatives. No longer was the Church under royal control. The princes of the empire were turning into independent sovereigns even as the towns were asserting their independence. Germany itself was on the way to becoming an agglomerate of semi-independent principalities.

Frederick would remain five years in Germany, although with his Norman, Italian, and Sicilian roots he could never feel at home in that country of fierce winters and savage landscapes. He saw to it that his son Henry, as heir apparent, was elected king of the Romans. He also formed a close working relationship with the Cistercian monks and with the Teutonic Knights, an order surviving from the Third Crusade, whose Grand Master Hermann of Salz became one of his most devoted friends. To offset the growing power of the princes, he attempted to ally himself with the lesser nobility and the towns. But in 1220, to insure the loyalty of his bishops, he surrendered imperial rights to them, and eleven years later the lay princes forced him to grant them equivalent rights, rights on which German unity would finally founder.

For the next thirty years, Frederick would be occupied chiefly with his long and bitter struggle with the papacy. To be crowned in Saint Peter's, he acknowledged that Sicily was no part of the empire, that it was held by him as a fief of the Church, and he swore that as soon as he was anointed he would resign that kingdom to his son Henry VII. His real intention was, however, to continue to rule Sicily and to let his son rule Germany, and with this in mind he had Henry made duke of Swabia. Gregory IX, Innocent's firm and able nephew, excommunicated Frederick in 1227, ostensibly for his failure to fulfill a vow to go

on the Fifth Crusade, but actually because Gregory was determined to safeguard the papacy by humbling the house of Hohenstaufen. When Frederick, still under the Church's ban, set out belatedly for the Holy Land, papal troops declared a crusade against Sicily. Even when the emperor managed through a treaty with the sultan of Egypt to reoccupy the actual city of Jerusalem, Gregory termed it an "execrable pact" and placed the Holy City itself under interdiction. Frederick, returning with an army of Saracens, Sicilians, and Crusaders, easily drove out the papal invaders, and in 1230 he and Gregory came to wary terms.

At the height of his power and at temporary peace with the Church, the emperor found himself faced with a revolt by his son Henry in Germany. Frederick regarded the German king as merely his representative. Henry saw himself as an independent ruler and much resented his father's bounty to the princes. Once before Henry had revolted, only to recant and secure his father's pardon. This time he

Adam and Eve partaking of the Tree of Knowledge, a panel from a painted wooden ceiling executed circa 1225 for Saint Michael's Church, Hildesheim

allied himself with his father's most determined enemies, the Lombard cities, who offered him the Iron Crown of Lombardy. Yet Frederick was so unconcerned that he did not even bother to take an army with him as he crossed the Alps on his punitive expedition. At his mere presence the rebellion collapsed. Henry was captured and would spend the next seven years in one prison after another, finally dying under mysterious circumstances. Henry's nine-year-old brother, Conrad, was elected king of the Romans and future emperor, after which Frederick left Germany in 1237 never to return. Conrad IV remained behind under the guardianship of the archbishop of Mainz.

The hostility of the papacy to the house of Hohenstaufen remained constant. The Hohenstaufens could not abate their claim for universal dominion; the popes could not endure it. Gregory in 1239 had instructed his bishops to publish sentence of excommunication against Frederick in all towns and villages with the ringing of bells and burning of lights. For the last eight years of Frederick's life, Gregory's successor, Innocent IV, waged a constant and relentless war against him. Yet though the pope set up two antikings in Germany, though (like Innocent and Gregory before him) he devoted his best efforts to undermining the power of the Hohenstaufens, he met with little success. At most he had scourged Germany with civil war, bloodshed, and anarchy. Time and again Frederick was placed under the Church's ban, and in 1240 half the bishops of Germany were excommunicated with him. Later the ban was extended to his children and grandchildren. The effect in Germany was negligible. Even the ominous new threat to Europe poised by the advance of the Mongols did not alter Innocent's determination. In 1245 at the Council of Lyons after being forced to flee Rome, he declared "Frederick of Swabia" deposed as a relapsed violator of the peace with the Church, guilty of sacrilege and suspected of heresy, and he preached a crusade against the "son of perdition," the "sometime" emperor, while offering the crown to Robert of France, to the heir to the Danish throne, and to Haakon of Norway. Frederick in turn denounced the pope as antichrist and urged the kings of Europe to expropriate the wealth of the corrupt Church. Imperial and papal factions, Guelf and Ghibbeline, fought each other with increasing savagery throughout northern Italy.

When Frederick died suddenly in 1250, Innocent's circumstances had become desperate. "Let the heavens rejoice and let the earth be glad!" he wrote in relief after hearing the news of the emperor's death. With Frederick, the last true emperor, gone, the papacy revived but the empire itself seemed on the point of dissolution.

Frederick's heir, Conrad IV, was only twenty-two and would die before he was twenty-six. He would never be crowned emperor, although he was king of the Romans and his father had named him king of Sicily in his will. Conrad was willing to come to terms with the pope, but as a Hohenstaufen he could not meet Innocent's indispensable condition of a separation of Sicily and the empire. Unlike the Italianate Frederick, he regarded himself as a German and the empire as German, with Italy as a subject province, a source of revenue. He had put down a rebellion in Sicily and was preparing an expedition against his German enemies when he died suddenly of malaria.

The following nineteen years became known as the Great Interregnum. Although rival kings of the Romans persisted during this time, none were able to restore the fragmented German realm. At first it seemed that Germany might be united under the papal antiking, the count of Holland, until he was killed in a skirmish not long after Conrad's death.

By this time a great change had taken place in the election of the king of the Romans. Earlier all the princes of the empire had taken part. In the election of 1257 that number was restricted to seven: the archbishops of Mainz, Cologne, and Trier, and four lay electors who held the archoffices of the imperial household—the count palatine of the Rhine (representing the extinct duchy of Franconia), the duke of Saxony, the margrave of Brandenburg, and the king of Bohemia. Since the electors of 1257 could not agree on a German prince, they divided on two foreign ones. Four electors—well bribed for their acquiescence—voted for Richard of Cornwall, brother of the king of England. The other three chose Alfonso X of Castile. Richard was crowned at Aachen, but his rule was fleeting and fictional in spite of the vast sums he expended to insure it.

With the central power inoperative in Germany, feuds and private wars raged across the land. Only the numerous self-governing towns, banding together for protection, survived as islands of peace in a sea of anarchy. A Rhineland League, formed in 1254, stretched from Cologne to Basel and numbered at one time seventy towns. Smaller groups proved more enduring, including that of Lübeck, Rostock, and Wismar, which would form the core of the great Hanseatic League.

Yet the chaos of Germany brought no halt to the eastern expansion. The Teutonic Knights, diverted from Syria, had pushed into Prussia, and all but completed the conquest of that northern forest land, establishing themselves, building great castles and fortified towns. Germans of every class swarmed into the opened regions—nobles, burghers, peasants.

Though the Hohenstaufen dynasty had come to an end with Conrad's death in 1254, his two-year-old son Conradin survived. Brought up in the court of his uncle, the duke of Bavaria, but king of Sicily by inheritance, he found his claim disregarded by Innocent, who for a time annexed Sicily to the Papal States. Manfred, Frederick II's bastard son, spread a rumor that Conrad had died and promptly seized the crown for himself in 1258. Pope Urban IV, in 1262, brought in the crafty and coldly ambitious Charles of Anjou with an army of mercenaries to conquer that kingdom. Charles defeated the Sicilians at Benevento four years later and Manfred died in the fighting. The Frenchman proved a cruel, grasping, and oppressive ruler. Manfred's former supporters and the remaining Ghibelline adherents flocked to Swabia to beg the fifteen-year-old Conradin to take up arms against the hated Frenchman. Precocious, brave, and ambitious, considering himself both emperor and the king of Sicily, Conradin did not hesitate. He entered Italy in 1267 with a German army and was welcomed by the cities of Pavia, Siena, and Pisa. Some months later he occupied Rome. Sicily flared up in revolt. In August, 1268, his army came face to face with Charles' lesser army at Tagliacozzo. But Charles, though inferior in arms, was superior in generalship. By a skillful maneuver, his rearguard succeeded in ambushing and routing the German force. Conradin fled and was captured. After a mock trial at Naples, and with the approval of the pope, Charles had the gallant boy beheaded.

CHAPTER VI

THE POPE'S RELUCTANT VASSALS

The Great Interregnum of 1254–73 was one of the dreariest periods of German history. Although Richard and Alfonso lingered as absent titular kings, it seemed that the very name Holy Roman Empire might soon disappear. The German princes continued to reinforce their positions as independent sovereigns, while the Low Countries came increasingly under the influence of France. Law courts in Germany ceased to function; the little remaining machinery of government was running down; town and country cried out for a real king to restore order. The new pope, Gregory X, was eager to see the Interregnum ended by a strong monarch who would help him unite Christendom in still another crusade. Richard's death in 1272 opened the way. The Hohenstaufen king Ottocar II of Bohemia, the most powerful noble of the empire, was the logical choice, but the other electors meeting in Frankfurt hesitated at choosing a monarch who might overpower them. Excluding him from the electoral council altogether, they awarded his electoral chair to the duke of Bavaria. Then the seven electors assembled proceeded to elect a relatively insignificant Swabian count of an old if not particularly distinguished Alsatian family, Ru-

A composite rendering of German towns serves as the background for this Dürer engraving of Saint Anthony the Hermit.

dolf I of Hapsburg. A shrewd, elderly man of solid character, a Hohenstaufen partisan, Rudolf was generally well-liked and respected. His coronation in 1273 in Charlemagne's Aachen with Charlemagne's crown thrust the Hapsburg family forward onto the larger European stage. Gregory accepted the election. Ottocar did not, insisting on his own electoral right and refusing to recognize the new king. Twice the Bohemian king attempted to revolt, but the princes stood solidly behind Rudolf, declaring Ottocar an outlaw. Persisting in his revolt, Ottocar was killed in battle.

Rudolf now felt free to embark on the general policy that later German kings would follow: the expansion of his house and the building up of the monarchy. Italy and the imperial coronation he considered minor matters. The duchies of Austria, Styria, Carniola, and Carinthia, confiscated from Ottocar, he now awarded to his sons Albert and Rudolf. This growing power of Hapsburgs made the princes and the electors increasingly uneasy, particularly when the king attempted to obtain the kingdom of Hungary for Albert and to renew the duchy of Swabia for Rudolf. The latter son died even as his father was trying to arrange for his succession as king of the Romans. When Rudolf I himself died a few months later, the electors refused to accept the rough and tyrannical Duke Albert of Austria, electing instead Count Adolf of Nassau, a brave and able man of small possessions.

In spite of his modest beginnings Adolf soon showed himself as zealous as his predecessor in expanding his authority. In a controversy over succession rights he sent his imperial troops to lay waste much of Meissen and Thuringia. When Philip the Fair of France encroached on the empire's western boundaries, Adolf allied himself with England to declare war. Affronted by his ambitions, the electors met in May, 1298, to depose him. Since Duke Albert was the only prince strong enough to overthrow Adolf, he was now promised the kingship if he succeeded. Albert's motley army met the thin ranks of the imperial forces two months later and Adolf was slain.

Though the electors, forced by circumstances, accepted Albert as king, the Hapsburg monarch remained feared and unloved. He was, however, able to come to terms with Pope Boniface VIII, who, having once denounced him as a traitorous usurper, made the full turnabout of confirming his election and declaring the king and future emperor to be the superior of all other kings. Albert in turn recognized the authority of the papacy and took the oath of a papal vassal.

Albert's downfall came after he refused a share of the Hapsburg inheritance to his brother Rudolf's son John, duke of Swabia. In revenge John and three Swabian nobles ambushed and murdered him on a woodland path. Although the murderers were banished, the electors wanted no more Hapsburg authority. Passing over Albert's son Frederick the Fair, disregarding even the heavy bribes offered by the king of France to advance his brother, they finally chose a minor count of an old family, Henry of Luxemburg. Count Henry, who thus became King Henry VII, had been brought up at the French court and spoke French rather than German. Upright, romantically minded, he thought of himself primarily as God's secular vicar, the emperor who would bring peace to a restored Holy Roman Empire. In his German kingdom he was practical enough, seeking like his Hapsburg predecessors to expand his house and, with considerably more success, to strengthen his royal authority. Through the marriage of his son John to the daughter of Wenceslaus II of Bohemia, he secured the crown of that kingdom for his family and made the house of Luxemburg one of the great houses of fourteenth-century Europe.

Obsessed by the archaic imagery of God's terrestrial empire—akin to Dante's *De Monarchia*—he marched to Italy with an army of Walloons, declaring he was neither Guelf nor Ghibelline but above partisanship. His dream was to be crowned at Rome, although at this point the papacy itself had moved to the safer environs of Avignon. Welcomed at first by both factions, offered a replica of the Iron Crown of Lombardy—the original being in pawn—he soon found himself caught up in the turbulent complications of Italian political rivalry. It was impossible to satisfy both sides. Soon the Guelfs turned against him, and he entered Rome to the accompaniment of furious street fighting. Unable to capture the Vatican, he had great difficulty even to get the papal legates to crown him at Saint John Lateran. Through an alliance with Frederick of Sicily, Henry was preparing to bring his other Italian enemies to terms when he died of fever in his camp near Siena in August, 1313. Dante lamented his death in the *Divine Comedy,* and in Germany he was mourned as the first ruler since Barbarossa to check the power of the princes.

Henry of Luxemburg's spirit harked back to Charlemagne and Barbarossa. But the emergent fourteenth century moved relentlessly ahead even as he moved backward. It was a time when the old feudal and scholastic world was beginning to decay. Manors were evolving into estates and serfs into peasants, while the peasants themselves were experiencing an unwonted prosperity as trading flourished and their produce was absorbed by the towns. Within the town the guild system had already attained its full flourishing. New art forms were developing. The rounded Romanesque was giving way to the Gothic, that art of the infinite thrusting up from the earth in its struggle against the limitations of space. The foundations of Cologne's cathedral had been laid in 1248, Marburg's in 1235, Strasbourg's in 1276. The climax of the age, to which the fourteenth century seemed to point, would be the invention around 1440 of movable type printing by Johann Gensfleisch (Gooseflesh), or Gutenberg as he preferred to be known.

Sometimes by amicable agreement, sometimes by bloody conflict—as in the case of Strasbourg and Cologne—the towns broke the feudal bonds that held them to their lay and ecclesiastical lords. With their growing economic strength they expanded their overseas trade. The Hanseatic League spread to include all the important ports from Amsterdam to Reval.

In France the king, by allying himself with the towns, had been able to subjugate his refractory vassals one by one and lay the groundwork for an absolute monarchy. The kingdoms of Spain followed the French pattern. In England the struggle of the nobles against the crown resulted in a division of executive power between crown and parliament. No such resolution took place within the empire. While other nations grew, the German nation sank into political impotence, in striking contrast to its economic and intellectual development. Power rested in the princes and the free towns. Certain families maintained their preeminence generation after generation—the Luxemburgs, the Hapsburgs, the Wittelsbachs in Bavaria and the Palatinate of the Rhine, the Wettins in Meissen and Thuringia, the Ascanians in Brandenburg and what remained of Saxony. So Germany's pattern would continue for centuries; an antination.

Yet the magic of the empire's name remained long after the content had leached away. The king of the Romans was still formally ac-

The Hanseatic port of Hamburg, with its crowded harbor, busy wharves, and bustling merchants, is pictured in the city's Municipal Code of 1497.

knowledged as the first of rulers, and the crown still provided a center of sorts. But the cessation of such campaigns as the Hohenstaufens had waged in Italy left the knights and the men-at-arms who had followed the emperors without a trade. Prices of goods and services rose with the new prosperity; the real value of fixed rents for domain lands declined. Chivalry found itself eclipsed by economics. One of the grimmer results stemming from the impoverished nobility and the unemployed knights was the rise of the robber barons who by the mid-fourteenth century had become the bane of commerce and the scourge of the countryside. Only the walled towns were able to withstand them.

The death of Henry VII took Germany by surprise. Renewed rivalry for the imperial crown between the Hapsburg Frederick the Fair, duke of Austria, and the Wittelsbach Louis, duke of Bavaria, resulted in the disputed election of 1314. The electors were at an impasse. Both Frederick and Louis claimed the throne, both had themselves crowned. A desultory eight-year war followed in which, although the countryside was ravaged, each army showed a marked disinclination to meet its adversary in the field. Finally in the autumn of 1322, after two Hapsburg armies had invaded Bavaria, Louis rallied his forces and with the support of King John of Bohemia met Frederick's challenge at Mühldorf. It was a battle that hung in the balance until a charge of fresh cavalry led by the burgrave of Nuremberg, Frederick of Hohenzollern, routed the Hapsburg forces. Duke Frederick and his brother were both captured along with some 1,400 of their followers, and their family cause collapsed.

Louis IV remained in possession of the crown. Like his predecessors he was concerned chiefly with the aggrandizement of his house. By tradition, vacant or confiscated fiefs did not revert to the crown but were nevertheless at the disposal of the king. Louis, when the Ascanian rulers of the March of Brandenburg died out, awarded this great territory to his son Louis, much to the chagrin of John of Bohemia, who had expected Brandenburg as a reward for his loyalty at Mühldorf. In Lombardy, Louis intervened to prevent the papal forces from overthrowing the Ghibelline tyrant of Verona, and the Visconti of Milan, thereby earning the durable emnity of Pope John XXII in Avignon, who after threats and warnings excommunicated him in 1324. The once-formidable ban had by this time lost most of its potency. Germany remained indifferent to papal fulminations. Louis countered by accusing the pope of heresy. Neither ruler could do any direct harm to the other. The final conflict of papacy and empire dwindled away into empty if belligerent phrases and claims without substance.

Louis had been politic enough to treat the defeated Hapsburgs generously, winning over Frederick's supporters by recognizing Frederick as joint king. When Louis found that the German bishops tended to side with the pope, he countered by leading an expedition to Italy where he had himself crowned emperor in Rome by four syndics representing the Roman people. His efforts to set up an antipope by popular decree ended, however, in failure and he returned to Germany, where he found himself faced with enmities that threatened his throne. Pope John had repeated his sentences of deposition, confiscation, interdiction, and excommunication, and now called for a crusade against the heretic emperor. The pope's death and the succession of Benedict XII brought no amelioration. Faced with growing internal opposition, Louis made outward placating gestures, even sending a delegation of German clergy to Avignon with the offer to renounce the imperial title, do penance, and go on a crusade. Only one concession he refused to make, and that was to agree that his election as king of the Romans required papal sanction. Since this was the fundamental concession, the one that the pope demanded and on which Louis could never yield, negotiations broke down.

To the electors, the pope's assertion was a challenge to their authority. Meeting in 1338 at Rense on the Rhine, all—with the exception of John of Bohemia—declared that they alone had the right to elect the king of the Romans, and no papal sanction or approbation was necessary; the pope's sole function being to crown the emperor. Yet for all their support of his prerogatives, Louis in the end fell out with the electors. Likewise his Hapsburg and Luxemburg supporters turned once more into enemies after his seizure of the Tirol and Carinthia. His plans for another invasion of Italy were countered by a papal bull depriving him and his descendants of their rights and calling on the electors to elect a new king.

This time the electors—minus the two Wittelsbachs—followed the pope's bidding by electing a papal partisan of the house of Luxemburg, Charles of Moravia, the ruler of Bohemia and grandson of Henry VII,

who was then crowned emperor at Rome. The German imperial cities and princes, on the other hand, remained aloof from the new monarch, derisively nicknaming him "the pope's errand boy." An attempt by Charles to conquer the Tirol was easily repulsed, and Louis' party held the upper hand when Louis died in 1347 while hunting. His death was fatal to the Wittelsbach cause.

Charles had already raised an invading army before he learned of Louis' death. Almost unopposed he now ravaged Bavaria, marched through Swabia and thence down to the Rhine to Mainz before returning to Bohemia. The Wittelsbachs and a few cities continued to resist, but most of the other princes and cities were persuaded by gifts and concessions to recognize the new ruler.

Dwarfing the succession of rulers and their tangled ephemeral history, the Black Death reached Europe in the year of Charles' coronation, being carried by black rats on cargo ships arriving from the Middle East. In this universal disaster that lasted from 1347 to 1350, a third of Europe's population perished. The Black Death's recurrence every decade or so for the remainder of the century prevented the regrowth of the population. In the convulsive agonies of the enveloping plague, medieval civilization itself expired in an atmosphere of despair and defeat. International trade fell off. Cities no longer expanded. Although wages rose because of the scarcity of laborers, the price of food rose twice as fast. For a century Europe would lie stagnant in the grip of economic depression. God's anger seemed upon the world, a feeling intensified in Germany by repeated earthquakes that shook the Rhineland. Bizarre religious manifestations found expression in roving bands of flagellants hysterically imitating Christ's scourging. More sinister were the persecutions and expulsions of the Jews in Germany, often initiated by the flagellants, who accused them of spreading the plague by poisoning the wells.

Though the Black Death hastened the end of an era, it gave no impulse to the birth of a new one. Yet Charles IV, however shabby his methods of obtaining the throne, was in a sense Germany's first modern ruler, the politician to replace the knight. His boyhood had been passed in the French courts, and he could speak French, German, Czech, and Italian with equal fluency. In constant poor health, austere in his tastes and in his private life, devious politically, superstitiously religious (a

Cologne, a center of international trade and intellectual activity, began the building of this, its superb new gothic cathedral, in 1248.

guileless collector of relics), he regarded the Holy Roman Empire as an anachronism and the German kingship a means to advance his house. Whatever patriotic feeling he may have had he expended on Bohemia. The German crown was in any case fast becoming a legal fiction. In theory the king was invested with the authority to promulgate the laws of his realm; in practice he had neither the men nor the money to enforce such laws. The royal domains had long been bartered away, and the scanty revenues at the crown's disposal were mostly from dues levied on the imperial cities. There was little else for a Louis or a Charles to turn to but the promotion of his house.

A man of orderly mind, Charles tried to bring some organization and system to the collection of principalities and city-states contained within the nebulosity of Germany. Since he himself lacked the means to enforce his decisions, since the imperial diet was a formless, lackluster assembly of scores of independent princes, he turned to the electors as the one body capable of bringing some functional unity to Germany. In his celebrated Golden Bull in 1356, which remained the constitution of the empire until its dissolution in 1806, he was able to establish a more orderly and efficient procedure for elections, at least for a time, although his efforts to make the concert of electors an indirect governing body failed. His bull laid down that the king of the Romans was to be elected by the majority vote of the seven electors: the three ecclesiastical electors, the archbishops of Mainz, Cologne, and Trier; and the four secular electors of the kingdom of Bohemia, the Palatinate of the Rhine, the dukedom of Saxony, and the margraviate of Brandenburg. Whenever the imperial throne was vacant, the elector palatine was to administer the empire. Eldest sons of secular electors were to inherit their fathers' principalities, which were now declared indivisible, not to be alienated to lesser heirs, and independent of royal jurisdiction. The electors themselves were seen as allies rather than subjects of the emperor.

For all his slight regard for the diminished empire, Charles was unwilling to abandon any of his formal rights. He insisted on an imperial coronation, arriving in Rome and leaving on the same day, to the derision of the Italians. On the way to Rome he assumed the Iron Crown of Lombardy; a year later he had himself crowned king of Burgundy at Arles, as had Barbarossa before him. In more practical political matters he placated the restive duke of Austria, Rudolf of Hapsburg, by investing him with the Tirol after the death of two Wittelsbachs, and by agreeing that if either the Luxemburg or Hapsburg line became extinct the surviving house would inherit the defunct one's possessions. Intervening in a fraternal quarrel, Charles persuaded the childless Wittelsbach Otto of Brandenburg to name him his heir. Thus at the death of the elector, the emperor acquired Brandenburg and Lusatia. By astute bribery Charles persuaded the electors to name his son and heir Wenceslaus as king of the Romans, to the dismay of Pope Gregory XI, who found himself not asked to confirm the election.

Whatever Charles did he remained Bohemian at heart, with his imperial capital at Prague. To his capital he invited Petrarch and other men of letters. He hired French and German architects to complete the cathedral of Saint Vitus. In 1348 he founded Prague University, the first institution of higher learning in German-speaking Europe.

Charles died in 1378. In the years before his death, he provided for his family through the distribution of lands and titles. To his own younger brother he gave the county of Luxemburg. To his eldest son Wenceslaus, already king of the Romans and future emperor, was given Bohemia and its dependencies. The second son, Sigismund, was made the elector of Brandenburg; the third son, John, became duke of Görlitz in Lusatia. For the first time in nearly two centuries son succeeded father without dispute or conflict.

Although Wenceslaus was only seventeen when he became head of the Holy Roman Empire, his years as king and imperial vice-regent had given him practical experience to offset his youth. A learned yet friendly young ruler, quick as he was shrewd, he governed Bohemia successfully for a dozen years. Germany, that amorphous entity, proved too much for him, as did even Bohemia in the end with its constant conflicts between the nobility and the towns. Increasingly he turned to the chase for relaxation, then to the bottle. He ended a drunkard.

His reign coincided with the Great Western Schism in the Church that followed the death of the Avignon pope Gregory XI. Italian and French factions each elected a pope to succeed Gregory; the cruel and autocratic Urban VI in Rome, and Clement VII in Avignon. Rival popes would anathematize each other for the next third of a century. In 1409 a council summoned at Pisa deposed both popes and elected the cardinal-archbishop of Milan as Alexander V to replace them. However, both Urban and Clement refused to be replaced, and the consequence of the Pisa council was merely to divide the Church still further by adding a third pope. Wenceslaus tried in vain to persuade the two other popes to resign. He failed equally in enforcing the Public Peace that he had promulgated. Germany's need for law and order he met with indifference. Royal power fell into such disrepute that even the king's brother Sigismund, who by marriage had become king of Hungary, turned against him. Finally, the Rhenish electors met to depose Wenceslaus. Declaring that the king had done nothing to restore order or church unity, they replaced him by the elector of the Palatinate, Rupert III.

Rupert's ten-year reign was one of honorable intentions and complete failure. Outside his own Rhineland, his authority carried little weight. Wenceslaus still asserted his kingship, but the Germans ceased to be interested in the rival kings, neither of whom was capable of restoring peace and order. On Rupert's death in 1410 the Rhenish electors returned to the house of Luxemburg and chose Wenceslaus' brother Sigismund. The other electors turned to Jobst, a Luxemburg cousin to whom Sigismund had earlier ceded the March of Brandenburg. Jobst died within the year, and Brandenburg reverted to Sigismund, who now came to terms with his deposed brother by guaranteeing him the rule of Bohemia and the status of a German king. In the summer of 1411 the electors again met and this time unanimously elected Sigismund.

A learned man as well as a man of action, Sigismund was a reformer at heart, though at the same time he could be savagely cruel. Where his brother had turned to drink, he turned to women. His greatest handicap was his empty treasury. His preoccupation was with the throne of Hungary. The kingship of Germany presented him with a task which he, too, in the end would find overwhelming, for the connection of kingship and empire spread the royal authority over an impossibly wide area. No traditional center of government existed. Nobility, knights, and towns by forming leagues for mutual protection and self-government made the monarchy increasingly superfluous. Electors in their independence could impose conditions on the king-elect and then depose him if they felt the conditions were not met. The failure

This scene of emperor and antipope (aided by Satan) crowning each other was a contemporary comment on the venality of rulers during the Schism.

of the king's justice gave rise to the vigilante justice of the Veme, those terrible secret courts that had begun as unofficial peasant courts to counteract the lawlessness of highwaymen and robber knights, but whose name had become a black legend. In the west the Burgundian power absorbed the adjacent imperial fiefs, while in the northeast the Teutonic Order foundered against Slavic and Polish resurgence. Little more was left to the monarch than the control of lapsed fiefs and the imperial dignity, the latter being well exploited by both the Luxemburg and Hapsburg houses for advantageous family marriages. One institution Sigismund hoped might avail him was the Reichstag, an imperial diet theoretically open to all the empire's tenants-in-chief. In actuality the Reichstag was made up chiefly of the princes and nobles of central and southern Germany, and was dominated by the electors. A number of towns had acquired claim to representation, but their numbers and voice were still insignificant. Sigismund would summon the Reichstag on several occasions in the hopes of implementing his schemes for reforming and strengthening the empire, but in the end these schemes broke down under the intransigent independence of the princes, who saw cooperation with the emperor as a subversion of their own position.

At the beginning of his reign, Sigismund felt there was nothing that would win him more renown, nothing that was more his imperial duty, than to end the Church's Western Schism. His early support had gone to the Roman pope, the notorious John XXIII, who was rumored to have poisoned his predecessor. Through Sigismund's adroit maneuverings John was forced to convoke in the city of Constance in Swabia a general church council, a meeting which brought together several hundred greater and lesser prelates and lasted three years. Its success in ending the schism by removing or exiling the three rival popes was due to Sigismund in his revived role as emperor and protector of the council. Nor could he fairly be blamed for the council's dishonoring of the safe-conduct given to the Prague religious reformer John Huss, who was burned as a heretic.

In his chronic need of money Sigismund had first pawned the March of Brandenburg to his loyal follower Frederick of Hohenzollern, the burgrave of Nuremberg. On a further payment of 200,000 gold guilders to Sigismund in 1417, Frederick was granted permanent possession of that distant march with the titles of margrave and elector. With the death of Wenceslaus in 1419, Sigismund also became king of Bohemia. His accession stirred the followers of the martyred John Huss to revolt. Essentially the Hussites demanded a reformed national church, and Wenceslaus had been far more willing than Sigismund to meet their demands. So wide and so deep was their support among the Czechs, so formidable the armies they raised, that Sigismund spent the next fourteen years in vain campaigns against them. Only by making a compact with the more moderate Hussites could he finally bring the Bohemian conflict to a peaceful conclusion in the conciliatory Council of Basel. Sigismund died in 1437, the last male of the house of Luxemburg.

Two candidates emerged as contenders for the vacant imperial crown: the youthful Hapsburg Albert of Austria, and the middle-aged margrave of Brandenburg, Frederick of Hohenzollern. In the strict sense the Hohenzollern was an intruder, for Charles IV had agreed with Rudolf of Hapsburg to a union of their two houses if one should become extinct. Sigismund's pawning and sale of Brandenburg robbed the Hapsburgs of that march, which Frederick soon made his own, quickly bringing the restlessly independent Brandenburg nobles to heel. Though he had latterly fallen out with Sigismund he seemed the leading candidate. But the electors, in need of a prince of wider territories who could protect the Eastern frontiers of the dissolving empire, unanimously chose Albert. For the next three hundred years the imperial crown would remain a Hapsburg possession. Germany itself would evolve within the framework of the two great houses of Hapsburg and Hohenzollern.

QVOD·IN·CELIS·SOL·
HOC·IN·
CAESAR
IVSTICIA
CLEMENTIA
VERITAS
TEMPERANTIA
LIBERALITAS
AEQVITAS
GALLIS
VNGARIS
ELVETIIS
BOHEMIS
GERMANIS
VENETIS
VICTORIA
IN·M
ANV.
DE
I
SEC
HONOR
MAGNIFICENTIA
PERSEVERA
GRAVITAS

CHAPTER VII

THE AGE OF LUTHER

The waning fourteenth century saw an end of the peasant prosperity characteristic of the previous two hundred years. The rise of the towns, the cutting back of the forests to add to the cultivated acreage, the availability of new land in the east, and the disintegration of the old manorial system had all combined to hasten the emancipation of the serf to the status of a peasant farmer paying an annual quitrent. Such rents had remained fixed, while the real value of money fell, and improved agricultural techniques vastly increased the yield of the soil. Most peasants grew prosperous, some even rich. Serfdom seemed on the way to extinction.

The recurring Black Death, though it marked the end of peasant prosperity, was only one of the many causes of its decline. In itself the plague denuded the land of laborers. Among the peasant proprietors there was a steady subdivision of holdings and the rise of a class of landless laborers. To stem any attempts by the workers to capitalize on labor shortages and thereby drive wages up, landlords tried to regulate wages by statute. The emergence of small territorial states from the ruins of the empire also bore down on the peasants, who suffered from

Dürer's allegorical portrait of his patron, Maximilian, shows the emperor aboard a triumphal car. Victory, Justice, Temperance, and Gravity attend.

increasing taxes and a more onerous and exact supervision. In many cases the peasant paid out two thirds of the gross product of his land to the landowner, the Church, and the lord or magistrate who provided him with military protection. With the more general introduction of Roman law, men who had always been ruled by local custom found themselves subject to an alien system that favored those above them.

Far from disappearing, serfdom now renewed itself, particularly in the east, where farmer-knights set out to force the peasants into bondage. In Prussia, Pomerania, Silesia, Brandenburg, and Saxony, the lords of the huge estates increasingly pressed the once-free peasantry into their service and reduced the landless laborers to chattels. Mere residence on the land, they claimed, made the dweller a serf.

In south and central Germany the peasants were not as badly off, and many of them had freed themselves from all feudal obligations. But the prosperity of one decade might easily be destroyed by war or pestilence in the next. Beyond the exactions of the local lords, the great princes themselves encroached more and more on the least of their subjects, restricting their hunting rights, subjecting them to military service, taxing their livestock and possessions, until finally the peasants seized flails and reaping hooks and rose in dumb, murderous rage. In 1458 peasants besieged the archbishop of Salzburg after he had demanded a tax on their cattle. Twenty years later the Carinthian peasants rose against the emperor himself in a rising that would have strong overtones of anticlericalism and radical social reform. A new and challenging spirit spread across the countryside, half-religious, half-socialistic, with the underlying thought that of the sons of Adam no man is better than the next. Peasants rallied under their *Bundschuh* banner depicting the peasant shoe with leather thongs. During the three decades before Luther's tumultuous appearance in 1517, Germany experienced at least eleven serious peasant revolts.

A similar sense of uneasiness was evident beneath the formalism of a Church much weakened by its prolonged sojourn in Avignon. Earlier there had been signs enough of a reaction against ecclesiastical wealth, worldliness, and corruption, the domination of high church offices by the nobility. There had been the Albigenses and Waldenses in southern France, the Lollards in England, the Hussites in Bohemia, in the wake of religious reformer John Wycliffe. There was the spreading influence of the Munich scholar William of Ockham, with his attacks on the temporal power of the papacy. Heretical mystics now appeared in various parts of Germany, groups like the Friends of God—made up of pious visionaries, anticlerical agitators, ordinary burghers, and ecstatic nuns—who attempted to reform the Church from within. During the last decades of the century, it was as if the apocalyptic Four Horsemen were again riding—this time across German fields ahead of armies that trampled the crops into the dirt. Bad harvests brought on famine; outbreaks of the plague were reinforced by the arrival of syphilis. Among the harried and fearful common people, the belief spread that the world would end on New Year's Day, 1500, at the mid-point of the second millennium. Meteors falling on the earth and comets streaking across the sky were regarded as portents of the downfall of Man.

Overwhelmed by the anarchy of daily life, many found consolation in pilgrimages. Plowmen would leave their fields, blacksmiths their forges, housewives their kitchens, to make their way to shrines like that of the Holy Blood at Wilsnack, where three consecrated wafers had been seen to drip blood, or to the visionary shepherd of Niklashausen, Hans Böheim, who claimed to have talked with the Virgin Mary. To the multitudes who came to hear him—until church authorities had him burned at the stake—he denounced popes and emperors, nobles and clergy, and declared that taxes should be abolished, that land, forest, and water should be made common property, and that even great lords should be made to work for a living.

In contrast to the anarchy outside, the towns—for all their at-times savage conflicts between guilds and merchants—were islands of peace and prosperity. Within the walls capitalism developed as trade expanded. Within those same walls the emergent humanist scholars flourished, as well as skilled handworkers. Schools for the young sprang up, and literacy—rare elsewhere in Europe—became almost commonplace. The Italian Renaissance, pushing beyond the Alps, combined with the Gothic to create new German art forms. In Nuremberg, Anton Koberger, "the prince of booksellers," set up a printing shop in 1471 that would house two dozen presses and make that splendid city Europe's printing capital. In that same year and city, Germany's greatest artist, Albrecht Dürer, was born.

In the turbulent currents and countercurrents of the fifteenth century, following Sigismund's death, the emperors played a negligible role. Germany remained a patchwork of little Germanies; 66 free cities, some 240 petty states, several hundred free imperial knights who were absolute monarchs of their small domains. Below the level of the seven electors were 50 ecclesiastical and 30 lay princes, often at war with one another. Yet even in Germany, where the emperor was unable to make himself the head of a national state, the general European trend toward absolute monarchy was apparent. More and more, under the absolutist guise of Roman law, the greatest princes were able to master the nobles and towns in their own lands.

As duke of Austria, King Albert II had been able to demand obedience from his territorial nobles and taxes from his own. Able, energetic, in the prime of life, a thorough German—and through marriage to Sigismund's daughter and heiress, Elizabeth, king of Hungary and Bohemia as well as emperor—he seemed the one man capable of reconstituting the empire. But though he summoned several Reichstags, he could not agree with the electors on any scheme of reform. Within one year he was dead of dysentery contracted on the Hungarian plains while rallying an army against the threatening Turks. With his death the unity of Austria, Bohemia, and Hungary broke up.

In 1440 the electors, preferring weakness to strength, chose the eldest Hapsburg, Frederick of Austria-Styria. As Frederick III he would be the last emperor crowned in Rome, and for all his weaknesses as a man and ruler he would reign fifty-three years. His coronation at Aachen was the greatest accomplishment of his first four ignominious years, which saw Bohemia and Hungary revert to native rulers. A military disaster ensued when he tried to assert his imperial and family rights against the Swiss. Then for the next twenty-seven years he withdrew to his estates near Vienna. He said himself that he preferred to conquer the world by sitting still. His chief interests were alchemy, astrology, and his collections of plants and precious stones. In indolent seclusion, he cared little about Germany's welfare, even less about the empire's. Yet for all his negligence he never neglected the acquisitive tradition of his Hapsburg inheritance, passively nursing the hope that one day the whole world might be subject to his Austrian-based family. His house and goods he decorated with the monogram A.E.I.O.U.—*Austriae est imperare orbi universo* (Austria is to rule the universe).

A merchants' reception in sixteenth-century Augsburg, a south German city whose riverine site made it a center for textiles and other industries.

Anna
Berhin
Mary
herwart
Conrat
im Hoff
Regina
lauy
Langenmantel
vlrich
lucas

Frederick consulted the stars and carved his monograms, heedless of the perils within and without his borders. The Turks' capture of Constantinople in 1453 opened a road for the Moslems into Europe, and the victors advanced into Belgrade, threatening to invade the Holy Roman Empire itself. Frederick wept at Constantinople's fall but left the protection of Europe to Matthias Corvinus, king of Hungary.

Within the imperial realm the princes and nobles warred with one another or against the free cities. Albert Achilles, the fierce Hohenzollern margrave of Brandenburg, led several thousand nobles against the imperial city of Nuremberg, then the leader of a league of Swabian towns, in an unrelenting war. It ended in a stalemate as the nobles could not breach the walls and the burghers could not protect the surrounding countryside. Conflicts of every sort kept breaking out all over Germany. The princes contended for prince-bishoprics for their families, while the impoverished knights, in their dilapidated castles, lurked like birds of prey, ready to pounce on the unwary trader or merchant and hold him for ransom.

Only mutual hostility among the electors prevented the deposition of the absentee emperor, who even in his retirement was tormented by his insubordinate nobles. At one point his brother Albert even managed to seize the archduchy of Austria, leaving Frederick almost without possessions until his brother's death. His one permanent ally, the one he counted on, was Time, which might sustain him and obliterate his enemies. The Wittelsbachs maintained their family hostility. But he could outwait them. In 1448 he signed a secret concordat with the pope by which he pledged the obedience of the German people in return for financial help and the promise of an imperial coronation.

When Charles the Bold, duke of Burgundy, was killed in a battle against the Swiss, his daughter and heiress Mary was already betrothed to Frederick's son Maximilian. In spite of the objections of Louis XI, the marriage took place, for Mary had given her heart as well as her hand to this engaging and energetic young man. Five years after her marriage, Mary died following a riding accident. Maximilian, raising what forces he could, had continued the war against Louis, but a few months after Mary's death they agreed to a peace which dismembered the Burgundian state. Flanders along with the county of Burgundy, went to Maximilian; the rest to France. The addition of these wealthy provinces to the Hapsburg inheritance revived the fortunes of the emperor in his last years. In 1486 he saw Maximilian elected king of the Romans, and although he was to live another seven years, the affairs of the empire now devolved on his son.

The title of emperor, little more than a name, meant much to Maximilian's archaically romantic nature, for he fancied himself variously as King Arthur and as a descendant of Hercules and of the God Osiris. A tall, hawk-nosed man of much charm, he was obsessed with the concept of chivalry and enamored of tournaments. Even more than emperor he liked to be known as the "last of the Knights." In his vaporous role of Holy Roman Emperor he regarded himself as a Caesar, and like Caesar, he determined to be remembered in literature and art. He planned to write or have written for him 130 books, although he finished only one—a romanticized account of his wooing of Mary of Burgundy. He also planned a giant stone memorial for the Cathedral of Speyer that was never cut, a bronze equestrian statue for Augsburg that was never cast. Since his predecessors, Augustus, Titus, and Constantine, had had their triumphal arches, he felt that he as Caesar must have no less. But as his limited budget could not stand the expense of stone and mortar, he determined on an arch of paper. That arch, a sectional woodcut for which Dürer acted as designer-in-chief, was printed from 192 separate blocks that together formed a rectangle 10 by 11 feet; a paper paean where all the world is shown paying homage to Maximilian, to nonexistent military exploits, to his personal accomplishments, his two marriages, his relatives. One of the curiosities of printing, it is indeed an allegory of the insubstantial emperor.

Denying the need for any papal coronation, Maximilian proclaimed himself Roman Emperor-elect of what was now the "Holy Roman Empire of the Germans." Imperial reform, urged by several electors, he saw as a threat to himself, although he was forced by his financial plight to agree to an imperial chamber, an administrative council of twenty to raise taxes and serve as a court of justice. During his reign Germany was divided into ten "circles" for military and tax purposes: Austria, Burgundy, the Upper and Lower Rhine, Upper and Lower Saxony, Bavaria, Swabia, Franconia, and Westphalia. The practical effects turned out to be slight.

The frontier county of Burgundy would provoke discord and strife not only between Maximilian and Charles VIII in their lifetimes, but between Germany and France for the next four centuries. The emperor's second and dynastic marriage to the daughter of the duke of Milan brought him into renewed conflict with France after the French king had invaded Italy. But Maximilian's extensive expeditions across the Alps, launched with much fanfare but little means, were insignificant and futile. In the end the French seized control of all northern Italy. Equally unavailing were his efforts to reassert Hapsburg claims in Switzerland. His defeat by the Swiss Confederacy in 1499 permanently assured that country of its independence.

Maximilian's lasting successes were matrimonial rather than military. After his daughter Margaret, affianced since childhood to the future Charles VIII, had been humiliatingly rejected by the young French king, the emperor succeeded in marrying her to Don Juan, the ailing son of their Most Catholic Majesties, Ferdinand and Isabella of Spain. In that same year his son Philip the Fair was married to Don Juan's younger sister Joanna, who was, after her brother and an equally ailing sister, third in line for the Spanish throne. Don Juan died six months after his marriage. In 1500 Joanna gave birth to a son, Charles, and that same year her older sister died. Philip the Fair died six years later, and when King Ferdinand died in 1516, the boy Charles, Maximilian's grandson, succeeded to all his father's possessions. Three years later Maximilian himself died, after having laid his hands on enough Spanish gold (in today's values about 10 million dollars' worth) to bribe the electors into naming Charles king of the Romans.

Frederick III's wishful monogram became a reality in the person of his great-grandson. For the twenty-year-old Charles at his Aachen coronation bore among his titles not only that of Roman king, but future emperor; Augustus king of Spain, Sicily, and the lands across the ocean; archduke of Austria; duke of Burgundy, Brabant, Styria, Carinthia, and Luxemburg; count of Hapsburg, Flanders, and Tirol; count palatine of Burgundy; landgrave of Alsace; prince of Swabia; lord of Asia and Africa.

Two years before Maximilian's death, an Augustinian monk and Wittenburg professor took a single step that would prove more eventful than anything in the emperor's eventful life. On All Souls' Eve, 1517, Martin Luther struck the spark that would kindle the Reforma-

tion when he nailed his ninety-five theses denying the validity of papal indulgences on the door of Wittenburg's court church. Such indulgences were then being hawked about the countryside under the auspices of the Hohenzollern prince, Albert of Brandenburg, archbishop of Magdeburg, who had determined also to become archbishop and elector of Mainz. In 1514 the elegant Renaissance pope, Leo X, had given him the appointment on the promises of 29,000 Rhenish florins. Part of this huge sum the archbishop borrowed from the Augsburg banking family of Fugger. Leo, to help his archbishop get out of debt, granted him the wholesale privilege of selling indulgences within his own territories for eight years. There was nothing unusual in this. From the time of the Crusades the sale of indulgences had been a common financial expedient. Albert agreed to send half of the money he collected to Rome to help in the building of Saint Peter's, the other half would go to repay the Fuggers. The actual retailing of these indulgences he entrusted to a shrewd, if crude, monk, Johann Tetzel. Passports to Heaven, the indulgences remitted all sins upon confession, and Tetzel even guaranteed the purchasers the state of innocence they had enjoyed in baptism.

An allegory of the dream of Frederick the Wise (asleep in his palace bed), in which Martin Luther is shown inscribing his theses with a gigantic pen

Luther, having come to believe that forgiveness of sins came only through faith in the grace of God, gave expression to his long-simmering indignation over indulgences in his theses. His efforts to bring about the reform of a degrading trade were, however, interpreted as an attack on the papacy. Pope Leo summoned him to Rome to answer to charges of contumacy and heresy, but Luther's elector, Frederick the Wise of Saxony, managed to have the case referred to the imperial diet held at Augsburg in 1518. Luther appeared before the diet with the elector Frederick's safe-conduct, but, remembering the fate of Huss, fled secretly when he learned that the pope had ordered him seized as a heretic if he did not recant.

France, England, and Spain had by this time achieved what were essentially national churches, but in Germany the Church remained under the thumb of the papacy until Luther's appearance. The sturdy Augustinian monk emerged as the man for whom the times had been waiting. All the resentment over the opulent papacy with its privileges and corruption, all the nativist German hostility to Rome, found a rallying point in his person. Impelled by his theses, step by step he evolved his own conception of Christianity as based upon the Bible and the individual conscience, and he stirred the masses to revolt against "the clergy, Lucifers' brethren, and their whole abominable sodomistic imposture, their saints and idols, prayers and confessions, tithes and taxes." Yet Luther was no political revolutionary. His new religion was to be based on class and faith, a singularly attractive doctrine to the German princes who would then be ecclesiastic masters in their own realm, as he urged them to be in his *Address to the Christian Nobility of the German Nation.*

In that and two other seminal writings, all written in 1520, Luther proclaimed the freedom of a Christian being, and the Bible as the ultimate source of truth. When a papal bull condemned him as a heretic, he burned the document publicly. The following year the emperor called the Diet of Worms—the first diet of his reign—to give Luther the opportunity to recant publicly. Luther, appearing there, refused any practical compromise, concluding his speech with his unforgettable: "Here I stand. I can do no other. God help me. Amen." He then left Worms. The emperor thereupon issued the Edict of Worms putting Luther under the ban of empire and ordering the destruction of his writings. The edict was unenforceable. Protestantism spread across Germany with the speed of revenge. Sheltered in the seclusion of the Wartburg Castle in Thuringia by the elector Frederick, Luther began his translation of the Bible into Middle High German, an act as important for language and literature as for religion, establishing as it did the foundation for standard and literary German ever afterward.

Luther and his followers unwittingly destroyed the Christian unity of Europe without, however, gaining the German unity they had hoped for. Their movement soon developed an iconoclastic radicalism that they would disown, at times brutally, as in Luther's condemnation of the Great Peasant War of 1524–25. In that desperate uprising, a hundred thousand peasant rebels died fighting against the "princes, lords, and priests," and over a thousand monasteries, castles, and villages were burned before it was put down. The movement would be further divided by the more rigid Calvinistic teachings spreading from Switzerland and by such anarchistic communal movements as the Münster Anabaptists with their threat to established society.

The emperor Charles had made scant effort to enforce the Edict of Worms, being far too occupied with his war with France and his differences with the pope. In 1530 he at last called a diet at Augsburg in an attempt to reconcile the Lutheran and Catholic factions. Five Lutheran princes and two independent imperial cities proclaimed their principles in the Augsburg Confession, but attempts at unity proved impossible. The Protestant princes and cities then formed the Schmalkaldic League for the protection of Lutheranism. Charles, forced by the Turkish threat to endure the league, saw Württemberg, Pomerania, Saxony, and Brandenburg go over to the Protestant cause. Sixteen years later the emperor with the help of Maurice, duke of Saxony, crushed the league in the brief Schmalkaldic War. Maurice later turned against the emperor and allied himself with Henry II of France and the German princes, forcing Charles to bow to the Peace of Augsburg, by which it was agreed that each prince should determine the religion of his own state. For the princes it was a political triumph. For their subjects it was an exchange of authority. The battle for religious freedom was yet to be fought.

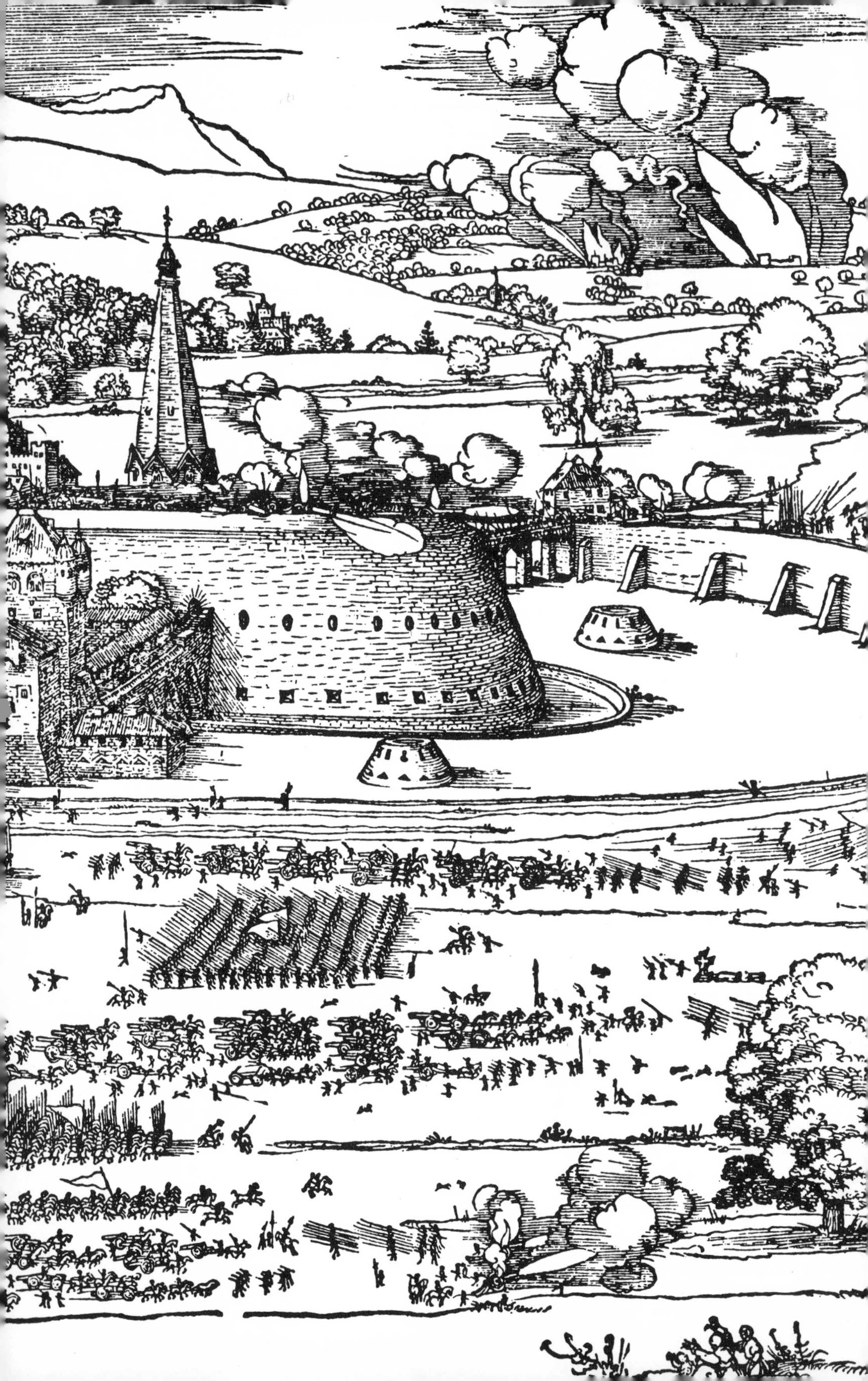

CHAPTER VIII

THE THIRTY YEARS' WAR AND AFTER

During the sixty-three years between the Peace of Augsburg and the outbreak of the Thirty Years' War, German Protestants and Catholics alike uneasily awaited what seemed an inevitable conflict. At one point almost three quarters of the German people had fallen away from the old faith. But in 1534 Pope Paul III began his vigorous policy of Catholic reform, reorganizing the Church government, purging the papal court of its worst scandals, and reforming the monastic orders. With the founding of the Society of Jesus in 1540, the pope was given a militant arm to advance the Counter Reformation. Much of the Jesuit effort would be directed toward Germany.

In 1522 the emperor Charles had made over his German-speaking possessions to his self-effacing brother Ferdinand, the archduke of Austria, the real founder of the Austrian branch of the house of Hapsburg. Ten years later Ferdinand was elected Roman king and was recognized as his brother's heir. When, however, the world-weary Charles abdicated in 1556, he divided his possessions. Spain and its colonies, the Netherlands, and his Italian territories went to his son Philip. The princes of Germany, fearful of the overweening Hapsburg power and

With the Reformation came a sense of nationalism, devastatingly expressed in decades of warfare. This woodcut is from Dürer's Treatise on Fortifications.

of what they called their "Liberties," refused to consider another king of Spain as Holy Roman Emperor, and so informed Charles. If the emperor must be a Hapsburg, the electors determined that he would at least be a German one, and they gave the imperial title to Ferdinand, who also acquired the thrones of Bohemia and Hungary. In Hungary he found his title challenged, but his most pressing problem there was the Turkish threat in the East that would haunt his house for generations. Unlike his brother Charles, Ferdinand was not vindictive toward Protestantism. His son Maximilian II, who succeeded him in 1564, carried that attitude much further, for he disliked Catholic Spain, read Luther's writings, and although a nominal Catholic, rejected the Church's last rites as he lay dying. Maximilian was, however, dependent on Spain for financial support in his struggle against the Turks, and he felt obliged to send his son Rudolf to Spain for his education.

Rudolf returned as fanatic a Catholic as his Spanish cousin and uncle, Philip II. Elected Roman king and king of Hungary and Bohemia he succeeded his father as emperor in 1576. Yet, although he brought the formalism of the Spanish court to Austria, Rudolf II brought little else, for his was a passive nature much like that of Frederick III. In his thirty-six-year reign he withdrew more and more from public life, content to dabble in astronomy and astrology, amusing himself with *objets d'art* and refusing to marry because he wanted no heir. When his energetic brother Matthias seized the rule of Austria, Hungary, and Moravia from him, he stayed inert in his capital at Prague. Finally a family conclave of Hapsburgs decided that he was unfit to rule and made Matthias the head of the family. In 1608 Rudolf handed the kingdom of Hungary to his brother. Left with only Bohemia, he was faced with a general revolt when he attempted to restrict the freedom of the Lutherans, who formed the majority of the Bohemian nobility. They forced him to grant a Letter of Majesty guaranteeing freedom of worship to the Bohemian estates and permission to build Protestant churches on royal land. The consequence of this letter would not be fully apparent until half a dozen years after his death, when the revolt of the Bohemian Protestants against the Catholic Hapsburgs would set off the Thirty Years' War that had been so long and so ominously in the making.

Historians have debated as to the ultimate damage of the Thirty

Years' War, whether a third or a half or more of the German population perished, whether half or more or less of the land was ravaged. Some areas, some cities like Hamburg, managed to survive in relative good fortune, but for the most part the war was a dismal repetitive chronicle of mercenary armies swarming across the land like devouring locusts, of sacked cities and smoking villages, above all of marching men accompanied by plague, famine, and sudden death. As the historian C. V. Wedgwood wrote, the war was "morally subversive, economically destructive, socially degrading, confused in its causes, devious in its course, futile in its result . . . the outstanding example in European history of meaningless conflict."

In 1609, the United Provinces, the Protestant northern Netherlands, had after their successful rebellion against Philip II signed a twelve-year truce with his successor. The end of the truce was seen as the outbreak of a war in which Catholic Hapsburgs would attempt to succeed where they had before failed and the Protestant rulers would seek to protect a free republic from extinction. But looming larger than any religious conflict was the rivalry of Hapsburg Spain and Bourbon France. In that fateful year, Germany—the conglomerate of interdependent states within the formal structure of the Holy Roman Empire of the German Nation—found itself the political center of Europe. The Spaniards wanted the freedom of the Rhine to transport troops and money from northern Italy to Flanders. The Dutch, and the king of France as well, sought German support to cut the Spanish lifeline. The kings of Sweden and Denmark each looked for allies against the other in northern Germany, while the pope attempted to form a Catholic Party in Germany to offset the strength of the Hapsburgs.

From the power base of their hereditary lands, the Hapsburgs had been able to intimidate yet not control the lesser German princes who, from fear of that dynastic house, opposed all efforts for centralization. With the linking of the Spanish and imperial families, the Hapsburg emperor was able to appeal to the king of Spain for help against those who defied his authority. German princes turned for support to the enemies of Spain, above all France. So bit by bit, Germany became a chessboard on which foreign rulers moved their pieces.

Unpopular though the Hapsburgs were to the majority in Bohemia, they at least kept a balance between conflicting estates and religious groups. The old and failing Emperor Matthias merely hoped that he might end his heirless days in peace. His wish was not to be granted. Two years before his death he yielded up the crown of Bohemia. Although the Bohemian throne was elective, the Hapsburgs had come to regard it as a hereditary possession and had selected the emperor's cousin, the fanatically Catholic Archduke Ferdinand of Styria, to succeed him. The Bohemian estates—nobles, burghers, and peasants—deeply divided religiously and mutually distrustful, voted reluctantly for Ferdinand since they were unable to unite on an alternative candidate. If he had not been urged on by his more intransigent Catholic advisers, his election might not have been challenged. But when he seemed bent on violating the Letter of Majesty, when Prague officials interfered with the building of two Protestant churches, a storm of protest united all the dissident groups in Bohemia. Fortunately for Matthias and Ferdinand, they were not in Prague when an insurgent force of noblemen, gentry, and townsfolk seized the city, surged into the royal palace, and, in what came to be known pedantically as the Defenestration of Prague, threw two imperial governors out the window. They, falling seventy feet into the courtyard, were fortunate enough to land in a dung heap and so survived.

A triumphant Protestant Assembly then gathered in Prague, appointed a provisional government of thirteen directors, and began to raise an army under Count Heinrich von Thurn. Shock waves from their revolt passed across Europe. The king of Spain dispatched troops and money to help his Hapsburg relative. Within a month a Spanish army had crossed the Bohemian frontier and another was making ready to follow from Vienna. Thurn's appeals for help were answered by the leader of the Protestant Union, the young Calvinist elector palatine Frederick V, and by the Hapsburgs' old enemy, the duke of Savoy, who together financed a Bohemian expedition of the duke's well-trained mercenary army. Commanded by the seasoned general Ernst von Mansfeld, they had in a few months driven the invaders over the border and were marching on Vienna.

While, at the death of the aged Matthias, the electors were meeting in Frankfurt with Ferdinand as their sole candidate for emperor, the Bohemians deposed Ferdinand as their king and elected Frederick in his place. Frederick, Germany's leading Protestant ruler as well as

Duke Henry the Pious of Saxe-Lauenburg, whose support of the Protestant cause earned him the admiration of painter Lucas Cranach

James I of England's son-in-law, left his capital at Heidelberg to take over the leadership of the Slavonic rebellion.

If he had been other than the vague, ineffectual man that to his misfortune he was, he might have built a permanent barrier against Hapsburg aggression from his Palatinate to the Oder. Instead he became the sorry "Winter-King" who shortly would lose not only Bohemia but his own Palatinate and die a rejected exile.

The sequence of the war became one of seesawing fortunes, with the ever-widening involvement of European powers, of battles lost and won without ever joining the decisive battle. Duke Maximilian of Bavaria, head of the Catholic League and ruler of the lands between Austria and central Germany, came to Ferdinand's aid with his army of 25,000 mercenaries under the command of the Count of Tilly. The plump and bibulous elector of Saxony, John George, in spite of his Lutheranism, rallied to the emperor, impelled equally by his hatred of Calvinism and his hope of territorial gains. At the Battle of White Hill, Tilly overwhelmed the Bohemian army. Frederick escaped to The Hague as a fugitive. Tilly's troops sacked Prague, the directors submitted to Ferdinand, a number of rebel leaders were executed, the Bohemian crown was made hereditary, and the land ruthlessly purged of Protestantism. From Flanders the Spanish general Ambrogio di Spinola marched to the Palatinate and together with Maximilian's army occupied it in a campaign of great devastation. Maximilian was rewarded with Frederick's title of elector.

From his Austrian power base Ferdinand saw himself as the reviver of a Germanic Empire, a power so strong that no nation or dynasty in Europe would be able to stand against it. What was for Ferdinand a dream, became a nightmare for the United Provinces, Scandinavia, England, and France. Christian IV of Denmark first rashly sent his army against the emperor without waiting for adequate support. Ferdinand, threatened with a hostile coalition, came to rely chiefly on the Catholic Bohemian nobleman Albrecht von Wallenstein, lord of 66 estates, overlord of over 300 vassals, whose unrivaled resources made him capable of recruiting and supporting an army of over 100,000 soldiers. As commander in chief, Wallenstein destroyed Mansfield's still-formidable army, while Tilly routed Christian's outnumbered Danes. In May, 1631, Tilly's forces captured Magdeburg in Saxony, sacked and then destroyed the city, and massacred the inhabitants in the most brutal action of that brutal war.

Fortune's balance, so heavily weighted in favor of the Hapsburgs, reversed itself violently with the entrance of Gustavus Adolphus II, king of Sweden. An ardent Lutheran and a military commander of genius, with a small but well-disciplined army, he won an overwhelming victory over Tilly at Breitenfeld, a village near Leipzig, four months after the sack of Magdeburg, and was hailed throughout Protestant Europe as the Lion of the North. The emperor, who had dismissed the too-powerful Wallenstein, now in his peril hurriedly recalled him. Gustavus Adolphus won another spectacular victory over Tilly on the boundaries of Bavaria; then in a battle once again near Leipzig, at Lützen, he drove Wallenstein's army off the field, but in this last great victory lost his life.

Gustavus Adolphus had received indirect support from Catholic France, where Hapsburg imperialism was more feared than the rise of Protestantism. After the defeat of a German-Swedish army at Nördlingen by an imperial army, Cardinal Richelieu as chief minister of France was forced to take direct action. In May, 1635, the French king declared war on Spain, and all connection with the original religious conflict gave way to political, dynastic struggles.

France was at first poorly prepared for war, and when Ferdinand died in 1637 it seemed that his forces and his cause might still be victorious. Under his son and successor, Ferdinand III, such hopeful prospects soon faded. Two young and vigorous French commanders, the viscount of Turenne and the duke of Enghien (later to be known as the Great Condé) occupied Alsace and, by defeating an imperial army, seized control of the Rhine. Enghien cut one Spanish army to pieces at Rocroi on the border of the Netherlands, then shattered the army of the emperor's brother, the governor of the Spanish Netherlands, at Linz. The Swedes invaded Saxony and forced its elector to sign a truce. French and Swedish forces swept across Bavaria. As the imperial fortunes waned, the German princes defected in increasing numbers. The prince of Transylvania overran the Hapsburg regions of Moravia, and finally a Swedish army besieged Prague. In 1641 the isolated Ferdinand felt compelled to sue for peace.

The Treaty of Westphalia that followed put an end at last to the torment of the Thirty Years' War. In the complexities of negotiations much of the map of central Europe was redrawn. France acquired the Hapsburg rights in Alsace, Sweden secured much of Pomerania. Swiss independence was recognized, as was the independence of the Dutch. In Germany the princes, who now held the absolute right to govern themselves and to make their own foreign alliances as well as to determine the religion of their subjects, were left as the only power to whom the disorganized people could turn. Estates and diets lost their authority, as did the weakened towns. Any possibility of German unification was now doomed.

The peace marked the end of Hapsburg supremacy in Europe as well as Hapsburg dreams of dominating Germany. The war of three decades was the last in which religion played a significant role, a role that dwindled as the war progressed, giving way to more contemporary feelings of nationalism. After Westphalia little more was left of the empire than a geographic term. Out of its disintegration, Austria, Bavaria, Saxony, and Brandenburg (the Prussia that was to be) emerged as self-conscious entities. The geographic pattern was that of a Protestant Germany to the north, separated by the valley of the Main River from a Catholic Germany to the south running along the axis of the Danube valley. Austria—the convenient term for inner Austria, Bohemia, and the appendage of Hungary—would recover power and prestige to become second in Europe only to France. The Austrian house of Hapsburg would remain the head of an empire of independent units, a league of German nations. But after the Thirty Years' War, it was clear that Austria and Germany were separate entities, even though Austria long remained the chief defender of German national interests. When in 1683 the Turks advanced to besiege Vienna, Austria took the lead in assembling an army of Austrians, Germans, Magyars, and Poles to rescue the city. Their victory was a reverse for the Turks that would end by seeing them driven back to the Balkans.

After Westphalia, the France of Louis XIV continued its expansionist drive. The Bourbon king's attempt to claim and conquer the Spanish Netherlands was thwarted by a formidable triple alliance of Holland, Sweden, and England. His invasion of the Dutch Republic five years later might have succeeded but for the stout resistance of the prince of Orange, William III, aided by the elector of Brandenburg.

Faced with an alliance of the empire and Spain, Louis was compelled to draw back, but by way of compensation he annexed ten imperial towns in Alsace as well as the old German city of Strasbourg and occupied much of the left bank of the Rhine. The French threat finally brought most of the German princes together, however reluctantly, in the Augsburg League formed by William of Orange that also came to include the emperor and the kings of Spain and Sweden.

Frustrated by the league in his attempt to seize the Palatinate, to which he laid claim as brother-in-law of the sister of the deceased elector Charles, Louis proceeded during the winter of 1688–89 to lay waste the Rhine with a vindictive destructiveness unequaled since the sack of Magdeburg. The Protestant world, already stirred by Louis's revocation of that landmark of religious toleration, the Edict of Nantes in 1685, was horrified and fear-struck at this wanton assault. England, Holland, and Savoy joined the Augsburg League, transforming it into the Grand Alliance. William of Orange, raised to king of England, became the main support and guiding mind of the new alliance. Eight years of inconclusive war were concluded by the Treaty of Ryswick, by which the French yielded up much of the territory they had occupied though retaining the Alsatian imperial towns and Strasbourg.

Far more significant than any other event in Germany after the Reformation was the rise of the house of Hohenzollern in the poor but strategically important March of Brandenburg. The first elector Frederick, who had received the march early in the fifteenth century on pawn from the emperor Sigismund, had found his primary task in subduing the insolently independent native nobility, the Junkers. Later in that century Frederick's sons, Frederick the Iron and Albert Achilles, turned from the then acquiescent Junkers to the subjugation of the towns. Gradually, ruthlessly, the Hohenzollerns consolidated themselves in the north. Another Albert, a grandson of Albert Achilles, became the grand master of the Teutonic Knights when they were at their nadir, and found in the Reformation the opportunity to disband the order and make himself hereditary duke of Prussia. Duke Albert's son and heir died insane, and the elector of Brandenburg took over the Prussian dukedom.

During the Thirty Years' War the land of Brandenburg was brought to utter ruin. The ailing elector George William, wavering from one side to the other, in Carlyle's words "on the whole did what is to be called nothing." Eight years before the Treaty of Westphalia, the twenty-year-old Frederick William, the founder of Hohenzollern greatness, who would become known as the Great Elector, succeeded the vacillating George William. Agriculture in Brandenburg had almost ceased to exist, the empty fields returning to bog and heath. In the electoral residence city of Berlin, the inhabitants had been reduced to eating dogs, cats, and rats. Frederick struggled to restore his land. A year after he became elector, he made peace with the Swedes by temporarily ceding Pomerania to them. He married the aunt of William of Orange, and, after the peace, brought in hard-working Dutch farmers to repopulate his empty lands. He saw himself as the embodiment of his country and people, and so the peasants saw him even if the nobility did not. With skill and imagination and tenacity he constructed the basis of a modern state. He sponsored enlightened policies in agriculture and commerce, created a paid standing army at the expense of the Junkers, even developed a postal system. He imported Huguenot artists, craftsmen, artisans, and merchants to Berlin, which he transformed from a village-town of 6,000 inhabitants to a city of 25,000. Though a Calvinist, Frederick tolerated Lutherans, Catholics, and Jews. He joined with the Dutch against the French invaders of the Palatinate, and when the Swedes moved into Brandenburg his peasants rallied to him as the father of their country and forced the invaders out. His victory over the Swedes at Fehrbellin in 1675 gave him his title of Great Elector, though after the Peace of Nijmegen in 1678 he was compelled to return some territory to Sweden. At his death in 1688 Brandenburg-Prussia had become the most powerful of northern German states.

His son, the frail, humpbacked Frederick III, was thirty-one years old when he became elector. Frederick's consuming ambition was to wear a crown, and since this could only be granted by the reigning emperor Leopold I, he eagerly joined the Grand Alliance and placed his splendid little army at the emperor's disposal. Frederick could not become king of Brandenburg, since the march lay within the empire, nor could he become king of Prussia after half that duchy had reverted to Poland. What he could and did become was king *in* Prussia. In 1700, Leopold, who regarded the matter as trivial, gave him the longed-for title. Frederick left for Königsberg, where with great ceremony he crowned himself as Frederick I.

The new king's aim was to make his court of Berlin a little Versailles, regardless of cost. French was spoken there and became the universal medium of correspondence. Frederick built palaces, such as Charlottenburg for his wife Sophia Charlotte, in the Versailles manner though on a smaller scale. He founded the Prussian Academy and the University of Halle. Teachers of etiquette, formal gallantry, and French customs were welcomed to his court. Tottering on red high heels, his hump partially hidden by the luxurious curls of his wig, he did his best in the thinner sunlight of Brandenburg to personify a Sun King. While he pirouetted in his Frenchified Berlin, his debts piled up. Watching the baroque pageant with surly detachment, his sullen heir, young Frederick William, a boy with the heart and mind of an army sergeant, bit his nails and bided his time. In what would come to be the Hohenzollern tradition, he, even as an adolescent, rejected his parents, detesting his foppish father, contemptuous of his elegant and probably adulterous mother.

At eighteen, Frederick William was married to Sophia Dorothea, daughter of the crown prince of Hanover. Of this young couple it was said that their job of producing babies "went on night and day." Several died in infancy. In 1712, six years after Frederick William's marriage and a year before his father's death, Sophia Dorothea gave birth to a boy child. The baby's umbilical cord was placed in a gilded silver capsule on which was engraved in French, *Frederick, Prince of Prussia and Orange.* Fritz, his parents called the infant destined to become almost as legendary in Germany as Charlemagne and Barbarossa, the future Frederick the Great.

CHAPTER IX

FREDERICK AND THE RISE OF RUSSIA

The years just before and after Frederick William's marriage to Sophia Dorothea in 1706 were shadowed by the War of the Spanish Succession, a particularly brutal conflict that resulted from the struggle between the Bourbon and Hapsburg houses for the Spanish throne and lasted from 1701 to 1714. When the childless King Charles II died, both Louis XIV of France and Holy Roman Emperor Leopold I maintained that they were the rightful heirs, both men being grandsons of Philip III of Spain, both having made state marriages to daughters of Philip IV, and both having negotiated numerous treaties that seemed to entail guarantees to the Spanish inheritance. Leopold intended to give the throne to his second son, the young Archduke Charles, thus reconstituting the long-time connection between the two branches of the Hapsburgs. But a month before Charles II died, he had reversed a promise to Leopold and named as his heir Louis's grandson, Philip of Anjou. Louis then proclaimed the young man Philip V of Spain and announced that the Pyrenees had now ceased to exist.

To this overweening French-Bourbon threat, the Grand Alliance of the emperor Leopold, England, and Holland responded with a declara-

A woman of Nuremburg, wearing traditional starched linen headdress and robe, from a series of pen and water color studies by Dürer

tion of war. The electors of Bavaria and Cologne sided with France, but the other German states including Prussia, Saxony, and the new electorate of Hanover joined the Alliance, whose two military leaders were the imperial general Prince Eugene of Savoy and the English duke of Marlborough. Eugene and Marlborough cooperated in their campaigns, attaining a singular trust in and reliance on one another. Their joint defeat of a French-Bavarian army at Blenheim in 1704 was a reverse for Louis that liberated all Germany from fear of the French. Marlborough's victory at Ramillies and Eugene's at Turin (1706), and their joint triumph at Audenarde (1708) brought the French to a point where Louis was willing to discuss terms. The 1713 Treaty of Utrecht, which confirmed the permanent separation of the crowns of France and Spain while recognizing Philip V as the Spanish king, was signed the same year that Frederick William I became king of Brandenburg-Prussia. The following year the elector of Hanover, a great-grandson of James I, inherited the crown of England as George I, succeeding Queen Anne, none of whose fifteen children had survived her. Hanover was thus united with England under one ruler, a union watched by the Prussian king with jealous and suspicious eyes.

Frederick William I was an avaricious, cruel, and upright autocrat with the tastes of a peasant and the manners of a boor, yet his accomplishments for his land were large and permanent. His great-grandfather, the Great Elector of Brandenburg, had prepared the ground; his father had elicited from Leopold recognition of the state of Prussia, the nucleus of modern Germany. Inheriting what was nevertheless a bankrupt state, Frederick William raised it to the level of the most prosperous, and forged an army that was the best in Europe. He reduced the Junkers to his obedient if privileged servants, and from the middle class created an incorruptible and efficient civil service. Serfdom still remained the condition of most of the subjects of his basically agricultural country.

The passions of his boyhood had been saving money and drilling soldiers, and these he carried over to his kingship. On his accession he sold off his father's jewels and gewgaws, discarded the elaborate palace decorations, and lived austerely in five rooms, to the disgust of his wife. French court dress went out, and with it the courtiers. The new king always wore a uniform and sword, and carried a rattan stick, which he would use to thrash anyone who displeased or disagreed with him. For his weightiest decisions he relied on his "tobacco parliament," a group of cronies and favorite generals that met each evening to smoke pipes, swill ale, and discuss affairs of state.

Of the new absolutist states, Prussia was the most absolute. Frederick William subjected his entire kingdom to a relentless central authority. Local tax collectors, granted enormous police powers, raised vast sums of money with scrupulous efficiency. Five sixths of Prussia's income went to support the army. Frederick William's one private extravagance was his Potsdam Giants' Guard of several thousand soldiers, all over six feet tall and drilled to respond like automatons. His agents scoured Europe for his guard recruits, and when these were scarce did not hesitate to resort to kidnapping. The Prussian king's army became the fourth largest in Europe—though Brandenburg-Prussia was only the thirteenth state in size—and by far the most efficient.

Frederick William liked to drill his own men. He reintroduced marching in cadence and invented marching in step. He also invented the draft. But he loved his army far too well to risk it in battle. Except for an insignificant engagement against the Swedes at Stralsund, his marching automatons never saw active service during his lifetime.

As he grew older the short-statured large-headed Prussian king became enormous, with a five-foot waist and a complexion described as "red, green, blue, and yellow." To the rest of Europe this 275-pound lout, with his perpetual uniform and his perpetual stick and his wild bursts of temper, was a comic figure. The Sergeant-King, they called him, while failing to realize the formidable efficiency of the autocratic state he had created, the grim potential of that unused clockwork army.

The young Fritz was as different from his father as Frederick William had been from the Great Elector. A gracious, blue-eyed child—though somewhat slow at learning—he had a charm of person and manner quite lacking in Frederick William. In later life Frederick II said that his father regarded him as "a kind of human clay out of which might be formed anything one wished." To the king's bellowing disgust the son showed an early liking for Frenchified ways, literature, poetry, and music. Frederick William determined to make a soldier of him. He regulated every hour of his son's life. When the boy was five he gave him a miniature company of cadets to drill, at thirteen he sent him into a guards regiment under the constant supervision of four officers detailed solely for that duty. Violent scenes occurred between father and son, the king frequently threatening Frederick with his ever-ready stick and at one time almost strangling him with a curtain cord. Behind his father's back the boy called him Stumpy.

When Frederick was sixteen he accompanied his father to Dresden to the court of Augustus the Strong, king of Poland. Augustus' court was the most elegant and profligate in Europe—Augustus himself was responsible for over 350 bastards—and it was on this visit that the inexperienced Frederick encountered two voluptuous females with an intimacy denied him in Prussia. It seems probable that from that encounter he acquired syphilis and that his physicians in their crude attempts to care for him left him mutilated and impotent. In any case he had no known affairs afterward. His marriage was never consummated. Outside marriage he would remain an ascetic.

As he left adolescence, the young prince's life became one of increasing misery. His father continued to humiliate and hector him, even striking him in front of his soldiers. Finally Frederick decided to take refuge in France, laying plans to escape with his devoted friend Hans Hermann von Katte, an army lieutenant. Before any real flight could take place, the plan was discovered and both young men apprehended. Frederick, lodged in Küstrin Fortress, was then forced to watch the execution of his friend from his cell window. For some time his father considered executing him too, or at least gave that impression. Eventually they achieved a reconciliation of sorts.

Frederick was a divided man, an esthete from whom a soldier would emerge, a son who hated his father and yet at the same time yearned for his affection. When he was twenty-one it was arranged that he should marry the pretty, superficial Elisabeth Christine of Brunswick-Wolfenbüttel. Married life at least gave Frederick a chance to live apart from his father.

The year of Frederick's marriage saw the death of Augustus the Strong and a contest for the throne of Poland between France and Austria that resulted in the War of the Polish Succession. Frederick William sent his son with a small Prussian contingent to serve under the Austrian commander Prince Eugene. In seventeen major victories Eugene had raised his country to the rank of a major power, but now at seventy his skill had left him. In that confused and shabby campaign Frederick at least learned tactics and coolness under fire.

From 1735 to 1740 Frederick stayed at the rebuilt lakeside castle of Rheinsberg, north of Berlin. Those five years, strangely unharried by his father, were the happiest of his life. At Rheinsberg he welcomed artists, writers, philosophers, musicians, and wits. He imported decorators and began his splendid collection of Watteau paintings. His hours were spent rhyming, writing essays, playing the harpsichord, and above all the flute, composing music, philosophizing, writing letters, particularly to his most honored friend Voltaire. French was the language of the court, and he strove to perfect himself in it. He spoke German badly and only when he had to, despising it as "ill-suited to eloquence and poetry." Yet beneath the dilettante, the transplanted Encyclopedist, there lurked the iron fist.

At Frederick William's death in 1740, Voltaire and the lesser intellectuals surrounding the crown prince hailed the advent of a philosopher-king. So Frederick seemed in those first joyful months, the most progressive and enlightened monarch of Europe. He abolished torture when it was still accepted elsewhere as a matter of course. He did away with censorship; as a freethinker, he proclaimed complete religious liberty for all his subjects. Farmers saw him as their champion when he banned aristocratic hunting privileges, as did soldiers when he punished those who had maltreated recruits. "Be advised once and for all," he told his inherited ministers, "that my only interests lie in that which may contribute to the well-being and happiness of my people." He meant it. One of Frederick's early acts was to abolish his father's Giants' Guard. But he in no way intended to weaken the army or diminish the militarism of the Prussian state. The philosopher-king, it would soon be apparent, was in his innermost core a soldier.

Five months after Frederick's succession, the death of Leopold's second son, who had become Emperor Charles VI, brought the male Hapsburg line to an end. Charles had sought through the Pragmatic Sanction, guaranteed by all the interested powers, to insure the succession of his daughter Maria Theresa to all the dominions of the house of Austria. But with the emperor's passing, the sanction was disregarded and his inheritance was claimed on complicated genealogical grounds by the elector Charles Albert of Bavaria, Philip V of Spain, and Augustus III of Saxony. The result was the reopening of hostilities at the end of 1740 in the War of the Austrian Succession. "This death," Frederick wrote Voltaire, "upsets all my pacific ideas; it means cannon, powder, soldiers, and trenches rather than actresses, ballet, and the theater." Although Frederick had at first seemed to side with Maria Theresa and had backed her husband, Francis I of Lorraine, as candidate for the imperial crown, he now swiftly and secretly led his superb army of 22,000 foot soldiers and 5,000 cavalry across the border into Silesia to occupy this richest of Austrian provinces. The suddenness of this seizure astonished Europe. Later Frederick admitted himself that "ambition, self-interest, and the desire to hear my name spoken outweighed other considerations and I decided for war." With Silesia part of his kingdom, he offered to give his electoral vote to Maria Theresa's husband. Without replying Maria Theresa mobilized an army and sent it against Frederick in the dead of winter. Taken by surprise, the Prussian king faced his first major battle at Mollwitz. It began badly. At the first charge the Austrian cavalry broke through the Prussian ranks, and Frederick, after desperately trying to rally his men, fled on horseback. Fortunately for him, the defeat was turned to victory by the cool competence of his field marshall, Count von Schwerin, who regrouped the Prussians and with iron discipline drove the Austrians from the field.

The victory of diminutive Prussia over the Austrian goliath persuaded Louis XV to form a secret alliance with Bavaria and Spain against Austria and to make overtures to the elector of Saxony and to Frederick. French and Bavarian troops soon invaded Austria and Bohemia, finally capturing Prague. With French support, Charles Albert of Bavaria was elected puppet emperor as Charles VII. Undaunted, Maria Theresa recruited a second army in Hungary and concluded an alliance with England. Taking the offense, her Austrian army now conquered Bavaria and drove the emperor into exile, while a second army advanced through Bohemia to besiege Prague. Worried by the Austrian resurgence, Frederick invaded Bohemia to defeat an Austrian army at Chotusitz, his second major victory. After this defeat, Maria Theresa felt it the better part of wisdom to come to temporary terms with the most militant of her enemies. Frederick was willing to wriggle out of his alliance with France in return for Austria's cession of Silesia, which was made formal in the Treaty of Breslau in July, 1742. So ended the first of Frederick's three Silesian wars.

Within one year the Austrians had driven the allies out of Bohemia, even as an army of Hessians, Hanoverians, and English under George II of England defeated the French at the Battle of Dettingen. Alarmed at the threat to his new province, Frederick concluded a second alliance with Louis and the fugitive emperor Charles VII. With an army of eighty thousand he forced his way through Saxony into Bohemia and captured Prague. The success was short-lived. Abandoned by his French allies, in the winter months his supplies failed and he found his army melting away from sickness and desertion, his treasury almost empty, and a hostile army threatening Berlin. After withdrawing into Silesia he regrouped his forces to encounter an Austrian army under the command of Maria Theresa's incompetent brother-in-law, Prince Charles of Lorraine, at Hohenfriedeberg, a name that would live in German legend. Although outnumbered, Frederick led the Prussians in person in a furious head-on attack that broke the ranks of the Austrians. His victory was followed by a second and bloody victory over Charles at Soor. Three months later a Prussian army marched into Saxony and, after defeating the main Saxon forces at Kesseldorf, chased the survivors over the border into Bohemia. Again yielding to the inevitable, Maria Theresa signed the Treaty of Dresden with Frederick on Christmas Day, 1745, giving up all claim to her lost province. Frederick's one concession—in which he again abandoned his French ally—was to recognize Maria Theresa's husband as the emperor Francis I, Charles VII having died. At thirty-three the Prussian king was at last left in peace and with his new title of Frederick the Great.

The War of the Austrian Succession dragged on for three more years, but at its conclusion all the signatories to the Treaty of Aix-la-Chapelle recognized Prussia's acquisition of Silesia. Frederick was given an untroubled decade which he used to build up his realm, doubled in size since the accession. From a Frenchified dandy, he had become the stern "Old Fritz" of his later legend, dressed always in his worn and faded uniform and old three-cornered hat. "I serve the State," he wrote, "with all the ability and purity that Nature has given me." He rose each morning at three or four, after five or six hours of sleep, to confront the mass of work that awaited him. He crisscrossed

his realm in all weather, probing, ordering, talking with everyone from ministers and industrialists to peasants and ordinary workers. His dearest relaxation was to play the flute. Some of his musical compositions are still performed.

During that peaceful decade, while Frederick was caring for his kingdom, his enemies were preparing to envelop him. Maria Theresa, even before the peace, had concluded a secret alliance with Russia's Czarina Elizabeth who detested Frederick. She was later able to extend the alliance to Saxony and then to France thanks to the influence of Madame de Pompadour on Louis XV and to Frederick's previous betrayals. "The three whores," Frederick called Maria Theresa, Czarina Elizabeth, and Madame de Pompadour. Sweden, moving into the alliance, posed an additional threat to Prussia. Faced with such an envelopment, Frederick in the summer of 1756 launched a preventive war, the bloodiest of the century, that would last for seven years. By leading it with an unflinching firmness and bravery he would in the end save Prussia from the extinction that at times seemed inevitable. By any count the odds were overwhelmingly against him both in respect to resources and manpower. What he did have was a central position plus the best trained and disciplined army in Europe. These advantages he played off with the greatest skill in six campaigns on the plains of eastern Germany.

At first Frederick's armies as they surged into Bohemia carried all before them, but at Kolín he sustained a heavy defeat that broke the legend of his invincibility. By the end of 1757 his situation seemed desperate, with the Russians in East Prussia, the Swedes and the Austrians closing in, and a large French army with German contingents coming from the Rhine. Frederick's capital of Berlin was seized and plundered.Then at Rossbach in Saxony the Prussian king, with vastly inferior numbers but using his memorable "slant formation," utterly routed a combined French and imperial army threatening Magdeburg. A month later he achieved an equally spectacular victory over an Austrian army twice the size of his own at Leuthen. Those victories made his name resound throughout Europe as one of the great commanders. To Germans, stirred by nascent national feeling, he seemed a successor to ancient heroes Hermann, Charlemagne, Barbarossa. Yet none of his victories could thrust back permanently the weight of the Grand

The new emperor and electors customarily dined together following election proceedings in Frankfurt's town hall. Here Joseph II is toasted in 1764.

 Coalition against him. Victories were always counterbalanced by defeats. His triumph over the French army at Krefeld would be followed by his worst defeat of the war at Kunersdorf where his army of 50,000 was reduced to 3,000 by a combined Austrian-Russian envelopment. "I have no resources left; all is lost. I shall not survive the ruin of my country," he wrote to a friend. In that moment he even considered taking the poison that he always carried with him. Then the fortunes of war again turned, giving him a belated triumph in 1760 over the Austrians in a great battle at Liegnitz and again on the bloody field of Torgau on the Elbe, the war's last significant battle. Brilliant though these victories were, they did not break the noose tightening around Frederick. The Grand Coalition still remained firm, bringing its resources together to crush the upstart king. Frederick in his despair again contemplated suicide.

In January, 1762, the Prussian miracle occurred. Frederick's implacable personal enemy, Elizabeth of Russia, died, to be succeeded by her simple-minded nephew Peter III, who nursed a vast if illogical admiration for the Prussian king. At once the new czar withdrew from the Grand Coalition, evacuated East Prussia, and even put eighteen thousand of his troops at Frederick's disposal. The French, already disheartened by their defeats in North America and their loss of Canada, were willing to withdraw from Germany as part of their peace with England. Only Maria Theresa was left. Realizing the impossibility of winning alone what she had failed to win with her allies, she accepted the mediation offer of Saxony's Augustus III and signed a treaty confirming once and for all Prussia's possession of Silesia.

Frederick, after six years' absence, returned in triumph to Berlin, acclaimed by hysterical thousands as the father of his country. But at the war's end, after the years of camp and bivouac that he had shared with his soldiers in all vagaries of weather, the 51-year-old king had become an old man, gray, wrinkled, walking with a cane, his digestion ruined. He still had twenty-three years to live, years in which he worked harder and longer than he had ever worked in his life to restore and renew his exhausted land. From state stores he gave his subjects corn for sowing, horses for plowing, money for rebuilding. He founded settlements, built canals, factories, a state bank, a state porcelain factory. Berlin he transformed with palaces and public buildings, though he himself preferred his more modest rococo Sans Souci at Potsdam. He reformed justice and education, set up the Prussian Law Code, to which even he himself was subject. Above all he traveled endlessly through his realm, inspecting, censoring, regulating, the first and most devoted servant of the state. No significant detail escaped him in the land of Prussia, of which he saw himself as the personification, the embodiment. The formidable bent figure in the shabby clothes and the three-cornered hat and the protuberant blue eyes was a legend long before his death. "Old Fritz," his people called him. His old soldiers called him "Father."

Old Fritz with his legacy of duty and discipline would become a German hero, his statue—invariably equestrian—gracing every major city. Yet he never regarded himself as a German. Culture meant for him French culture. The proceedings of his Prussian Academy were conducted in French. Though he had once graciously received the aged Bach, though he admired Handel, he considered German speech, German literature, and German art contemptible. The awareness of Germanness and German thought that was developing in Germany, that was felt with such sensitivity by Goethe and Herder and their friends, and that would in the decades to come lead the way to political nationalism, had no meaning for him. In an article on German literature that he wrote (in French) six years before his death, he failed even to mention Klopstock, Lessing, and Wieland. Goethe's stormy nationalistic *Goetz von Berlichingen* he found an "abominable imitation" of Shakespeare's "bizarre aberrations." Goethe's *Sesenheim Lyrics,* as much of a landmark in the renewal of the German language and spirit as Luther's Bible translations, was beyond his ken.

Frederick could see no farther than Prussia. But he feared for his country after his death. He warned that an indolent ruler could ruin the state in thirty years. In actual fact it would take only twenty.

CHAPTER X

THE NORTH GERMAN CONFEDERATION

Maria Theresa, archduchess of Austria, queen of Bohemia and Hungary, wife of an emperor whose powers were limited to conferring titles, legitimizing bastards, and granting respite to debtors, never wavered in her detestation of Frederick the Great. Ironically, the Prussian soldier-king became the hero and model of her son Joseph II. Joseph's ambition was to be a Hapsburg Frederick, to unite the sprawling dominions of the house of Austria into an efficient military state through which he would then transform the figment of the Holy Roman Empire once more into fact. Joseph was elected emperor after his father's death in 1765. For fifteen years he was coregent with his mother, and it was she who held the reins of government.

Only by combining with Frederick the Great to divide Poland was Joseph able to loosen those reins. On the death of the Polish king, Augustus III, two rivals for the throne appeared, one backed by the French and later the Turks, the other by Catherine II of Russia. After the Turks had rashly declared war on Russia, Catherine's forces so overwhelmed them that Austria took alarm. It was at this point that Frederick the Great suggested to Joseph—who enthusiastically agreed

The evolution of the German state altered life only slowly. Eighteenth-century peasants worked and played much like those depicted earlier by Dürer.

—and later to Catherine that they would all do better by slicing up Poland among them than by making war on one another. Their agreement resulted in the First Partition of 1772 by which Poland lost a third of its territory and half its inhabitants. Austria gained Galicia, Red Russia, and Podolia. Catherine took the largest slice in annexing Byelorussia, or White Russia, while Frederick by seizing what would later be known as the Polish Corridor (excepting the cities of Thorn and Danzig) was able to unite Brandenburg with Prussia. Maria Theresa opposed the partition as unjust and immoral. Signing the treaty, she predicted that "when I am long dead, the world will rue this day."

Frederick was almost a decade in his grave when the second partition of Poland took place, during the nine-year reign of his nephew and successor Frederick William II. In 1793 with the flimsiest of political pretexts Catherine and Frederick William further encroached on what was left of Poland, Frederick William seizing Thorn and Danzig and Great Poland with its million inhabitants, while Catherine absorbed most of Lithuania and the western Ukraine. In the following year a Polish national uprising led by Thaddeus Kosciusko was put down by Russian and Prussian forces. Then Catherine and Frederick William, this time joined by the last of the Holy Roman Emperors, Francis II, proceeded to eliminate the remnants of the Polish state. Warsaw and the surrounding country east of the Vistula went to Prussia; Austria obtained the Cracow region; Russia the rest of the Ukraine.

Prussia's Polish engorgement was the one decisive act in Frederick William II's negative reign. Frederick the Great had been the father of his country; his nephew was merely a womanizer. "There will be a merry life of it at court," Frederick had predicted with sad accuracy a year before his death, as he observed his incompetent heir. "My nephew will squander the treasure and allow the army to degenerate. The women will then govern and the state will go to rack and ruin."

At first, after the sternly regulative Frederick, the affable, lax Frederick William was welcome, as an end to austerity is always welcome. But within half a year his popularity had ebbed. This do-nothing king, incapable even of thought, surrounded by whores, schemers, and sycophants, soon became an object of general contempt. A visiting Frenchman noted that the ruler "hates nothing and scarcely loves anything; his only aversions are people of the mind and intellect. In the royal household, utter confusion reigns supreme. . . . No paper is in order, no petition is answered; the king never opens a letter himself, as no human power could induce him to read forty lines at a time."

Frederick William's chief mistress and the real ruler of Prussia was a trumpeter's daughter, Wilhelmina Encke, whom he had acquired when she was fourteen and later ennobled as Countess von Lichtenau. He was married twice for dynastic reasons, the first marriage ending in divorce, and in addition he contracted two bigamous morganatic marriages. General Bischoffswerder, who supplied him with reputedly sex-stimulating drugs, was in charge of foreign policy. Finances and internal policy were decided by a renegade pastor, Johann Wollner.

It was Bischoffswerder who was chiefly responsible for the alliance of Prussia with Austria against Revolutionary France, urged on by French émigrés who had fled to Germany after the fall of the Bastille. In April, 1792, the Legislative Assembly in Paris responded with a declaration of war. A small Prussian-Austrian army marched into France in the summer of that year, the leaders convinced that in a France riven by dissension it would be relatively easy to "smash those lawyers in Paris." Rusty from neglect, the confident but incompetent army started out from Coblenz, crossed into France, captured Verdun, and seemed on the high road to Paris. The illusion was shattered at Valmy, one hundred miles east of Paris, when they were met with the full force of French field artillery. In that foggy engagement the Prussian-Austrian army was not so much defeated as bereft of its will to fight when brought up short against the Revolutionary French *élan*. Goethe, observing the battle as an aide to the duke of Weimar, concluded that the day of Valmy "marks the beginning of a new era in world history." The poet's words were more prophetic than he realized, for even as the dispirited Prussians and Austrians fell back, the National Convention in Paris abolished the monarchy. Counterattacking, the French advanced to the Rhine, and seized Austria's Belgian provinces.

Germany on the eve of the French Revolution was fragmented into almost two thousand separate territories, some of them independent states and European powers, but most of them inconsequential midget domains. The mass of the population was badly governed, poor, ignorant, and helpless. Yet a feeling of change was in the air, a feeling part intellectual, part national. Immanuel Kant, the great philosopher

of Königsberg, sensed that he was experiencing an age in the process of enlightenment. The French Revolution and the Napoleonic aftermath would transform Germany even more than France, though in a curiously passive way. Only in 1813, in that last act of Revolutionary drama, would the Germans play an active role. More by chance than by intent would it fall on Prussia to give the German nation its modern political form.

When Frederick William died in 1797 he was succeeded by his son Frederick William III, a high-minded, if narrow, young man whose first acts as ruler were to banish the sycophants of his father's court and to arrest Countess von Lichtenau. Unfortunately for the new king and for his country, he was vacillating to the point of inaction. Whatever character his reign attained came through the charm and forthright patriotism of his saintly queen, Louise.

The execution of Louis XVI had brought about the First Coalition

against France. Spurred by England's prime minister, William Pitt, Holland, Spain, Portugal, the Papal States, Russia, Sardinia, Naples, Prussia, Austria, and most of the German states of the empire drew together against the Revolutionary French threat. However, when France declared war, the brunt of the fighting fell on Austria and Prussia. In 1795 the Prussian king, distrustful as always of Austria and faced with a bankrupt state, made a separate peace with France. Austria followed suit two years later. For the next decade, as the French under Napoleon came to dominate central Europe, Prussia would maintain a pallid neutrality hoping to ride out the storm.

Though the emperor Francis participated in the two subsequent allied coalitions and sent army after army against France, Austria was in the end too weak to stand up against the huge French levies and the military tactics of Napoleon. Austria's cession of the left bank of the Rhine under the threat of a French invasion was the beginning of the

Birthplace of Beethoven and seat of a university, eighteenth-century Bonn was a prosperous provincial capital clustered around this market place.

end for the empire. German rulers who had lost territories beyond the Rhine compensated themselves by taking over ecclesiastic domains and seizing imperial cities and petty principalities within Germany. At the 1803 Diet of the Empire, the rotting feudal structure further disintegrated as 112 imperial states were absorbed by larger states. After Napoleon's great victory at Austerlitz in 1805, he rewarded his client states of Bavaria, Württemberg, and Baden with Austrian territories, then established the Confederation of the Rhine under his protection with these and thirteen lesser states, all of whom seceded from the empire. When in 1805 Austria and Russia undertook one more campaign to check Napoleonic expansion, the armies of the Rhine Confederation fought for France. Francis II had already assumed the title of first emperor of Austria. In August, 1806, he at last recognized the obsoleteness of his ancient imperial title and set aside the imperial crown, bringing to an end the thousand-year Holy Roman Empire.

The disappearance of the empire was followed that same year by the collapse of Prussia. When the temporizing Frederick William, goaded by his advisers, at last demanded the withdrawal of French troops from his frontiers, Napoleon responded with a lightning attack. The Prussian army, resting on the mouldering laurels of Frederick the Great, whose superannuated generals still retained their command, was capable of only fleeting resistance. At Jena and again at Auerstedt, the French quickly broke the Prussian ranks and the Prussian discipline. Prussian fortress garrisons then surrendered ignominiously, the king fled to Königsberg, and Napoleon entered Berlin to be greeted with fawning submission by the officials who had remained there.

Napoleon's terms were so harsh and his territorial demands so large that Frederick William in despair allied himself with Alexander I of Russia to continue the war. But Napoleon's defeat of the Russians at Friedland forced them back within their borders and brought Alexander hurriedly to the peace table without regard for his Prussian ally. The French emperor and the czar met on a raft in the Neman River to arrange what would become the Peace of Tilsit, while Frederick William sat disconsolately on the riverbank. By the peace terms Napoleon seized all the Prussian lands between the Rhine and the Elbe for his kingdom of Westphalia. Prussia also had to give up the lands taken from Poland, now reconstituted as the French-dominated duchy of

Warsaw. Frederick William lost half of his possessions, and Napoleon would have wiped Prussia off the map but for Alexander's plea that it remain as a buffer state between them.

The states forming the Confederation of the Rhine expanded in territory while remaining cordially subservient to Napoleon. But in truncated Prussia, impoverished by the burden of indemnities, men began to dream of liberation from the French yoke, of a new German nation-state. Even under Frederick William, outstanding reformers like Baron vom Stein and Prince von Hardenberg chose to serve the Prussian state, even as the great soldier reformers, General Scharnhorst and Count von Gneisenau, reshaped and renewed the army. In Berlin during 1807 while the king still remained in Königsberg, the nationalist philosopher Johann Gottlieb Fichte stirred the hearts and minds of his compatriots with his *Addresses to the German Nation*. Stein, whom Frederick William privately considered "refractory, stubborn, and disobedient," but whom Queen Louise admired and encouraged, abolished serfdom and aristocratic land privileges, did away with class distinctions in regard to trades and occupations, reformed taxes, freed industry from burdensome regulations, and granted local self-government to cities and towns. Stein's chief aim was to arouse a new patriotic spirit among all Germans. Napoleon, responding to Stein's hostility, insisted on his dismissal and he fled to Russia.

Stein was a member of an army reform commission headed by Major General von Scharnhorst, a peasant's son who had risen to become the leading military figure in the Prussian state. Left with the miniscule army allowed by Napoleon, Scharnhorst remodeled it from top to bottom to make it into a potential major force, doing away with the Frederickian brutality, abolishing corporal punishment, opening the aristocratic officers' corps to any soldier of talent, and paving the way for a citizen army in a future struggle against the French emperor.

Patriots like Scharnhorst and Gneisenau wanted to unite with Russia against Napoleon, but neither the Prussian Frederick William nor the Austrian Francis was ready to take such a step. When Napoleon, increasingly distrustful of Russia, prepared for his invasion of 1812, Austria contributed 30,000 soldiers, and Prussia its whole army of 20,000, to his Grand Army. That army of 600,000 men, made up of Germans, Italians, Poles, Swiss, and Dutch, with only a minority of

French, was the greatest army the world had ever seen and one of the most ill-fated. Of those glittering regiments that crossed the Neman in June, only a sixth would survive the winter retreat from Moscow.

Napoleon's image as well as his Grand Army was shattered on the snowbound retreat. Even as the campaign began, the Prussian general, Hans Yorck von Wartenburg, in the Baltic provinces led his contingent out of the French service and proclaimed his neutrality. His act of patriotic disobedience set off a wave of national feeling that swept through Prussia, carrying the reluctant king along with it. After leaving Berlin for Breslau, Frederick William, impelled by popular enthusiasm and by such leaders as Scharnhorst and Gneisenau, issued an appeal to his people to form volunteer corps. Young men, the students foremost among them, rushed to the colors. Their teachers followed. The Breslau professor Henrik Steffens in a fiery address urged his students to join the free corps, then stepped from his lectern to go with them. In 1813 Frederick William signed an offensive-defensive alliance with Russia—soon joined by England and Sweden. Prussia's War of Liberation had begun, a war which seemed to the young men, to the freedom poets, Arnim, Kleist, Arndt, and Körner who died in action, to herald a dreamed-of German nation, "a golden future that lies be-

Louis II of Bavaria ruled bizarrely over a Wagnerian-styled court. Here the nineteenth-century king takes an eighteenth-century sleigh ride by moonlight.

fore us." Austria, under Metternich, held back for several months and battles, joining the anti-French alliance out of calculation rather than enthusiasm.

Following his Russian debacle, Napoleon brought a new army of 180,000 men into Germany, but they were not the equal of the old. After several inconclusive engagements, the armies of Prussia, Russia, and Austria converged on the French at Leipzig. There, in a tremendous four-day battle called by the Germans the Battle of the Nations, the victor of Austerlitz saw his sun set. Napoleon's defeat, his heavy loss of men, drove him back across the French borders. The members of the Confederation of the Rhine had by now deserted him. After a series of futile delaying actions that ended in the victorious entry of the allies into Paris on March 31, 1814, he abdicated unconditionally and was exiled to Elba. He escaped eleven months later, while the victors were parceling out their winnings in the restoration gaiety of the Congress of Vienna. His rallying of the French to him, his desperate but unsuccessful last throw of the dice on the plain of Waterloo, was followed by that vague declaration of Christian principles, the Holy Alliance of Russia, Prussia, and Austria.

Idealistic young volunteers for the War of Liberation had expected that Napoleon's downfall would see the princes of the old empire replaced by a unified German nation. But the powers at Vienna, under the leadership of the subtle, reactionary Metternich, were concerned with the establishment of a balance of power in Europe and the preservation of the existing monarchical order. Rather than a German nation, the congress evolved a loose Germanic Confederation—an improved if limited version of the Holy Roman Empire—with a federal diet that met at Frankfurt. The confederation was not a state, but an association of thirty-nine monarchical states and four free cities, with Austria as its hereditary president. Frederick William had wished to annex all of Saxony, but Austrian and British opposition restricted him to the northern half. Prussia in the settlement recovered the territories east of the Elbe, including Great Poland, and received much of Westphalia as well as Swedish Pomerania and the Rhineland. Although there was a united German demand for the return of Alsace, this province was left to France on the insistence of Russia and England.

Disappointing as the confederation was to the nationalists, it did give the Germans an elementary sense of unity and a developing national cohesion. If men like Stein and Gneisenau had had their way, Prussia might have assumed the leadership of a national movement in Germany. But their way was not Frederick William's, as he soon showed by the dismissal of his reformist officials. The students, in their zeal for what the Prussian field marshal Blücher had called "freedom and fatherland," now formed patriotic associations and took to the streets to demonstrate against the impositions of royal authority. In 1819 the murder of the reactionary playwright August von Kotzebue by a theological student provided the impulse and the excuse for Metternich and Frederick William to sign the Carlsbad Decrees, by which they agreed to suppress all manifestations of liberal nationalism and popular representation. Patriots like Arndt fled their native land. Even Fichte's speeches were banned from circulation.

About all that the Prussian people gained from the War of Liberation was universal military service. Metternich, for whom the new ideas of nationalism and popular government were anathema, dictated policy in Berlin as well as in Vienna. Prussia reverted to an eighteenth-century absolutism in which the king, the army, and the Junker aristocrats wielded a complete and arbitrary authority. What Gneisenau had hoped for, a "model state, thrice glorified by those things which alone aid a people in achieving progress: fame in war, constitution and law, and care for the arts and sciences," was by the time of Frederick William's death in 1840 no more than a police state.

The new king, Frederick William IV, was forty-five when he came to the throne. His father had been an indecisive autocrat; the son was a romantic whose mind harked back to the Middle Ages. A loquacious man, the first Prussian ruler to declare himself king "by the grace of God," he early announced his opposition to any written constitution, informing his questioning subjects that this sort of thing "destroys the natural relation between prince and people." Determined to hunt down those he considered subversive, he even removed from his post the birdlike professor and librarian Hoffmann von Fallersleben, composer of *Deutschland, Deutschland über Alles*.

The revolutionary wave of 1848, which deposed France's Louis Philippe and exiled Metternich, almost toppled Frederick William. Under their black-red-gold flag, democratic revolutionaries seized control of Berlin, demanding the freedoms that the volunteers of the War of Liberation had thought they were fighting for. Bowing to the temporarily inevitable, the king capitulated. A black-red-gold ribbon on his sleeve, he acceded to all their demands. "I wish only for Germany's freedom, Germany's unity, and order," he told them rhetorically, raising his arm heavenward. Other state governments in Germany were overthrown. Yet the revolution itself was essentially bourgeois. Marx's Communist Manifesto of that year struck little response in German hearts. The traditional forces soon recovered their poise and their strength, as did Frederick William, backed by his army. When a German National Assembly meeting in Frankfurt-am-Main finally produced a constitution for a new empire in which the power would rest in the people and offered the crown to the king of Prussia, he refused "to pick up a crown from the gutter," wrecking another dream of a united Germany. Frederick William did agree to a constitution of sorts with a bicameral Prussian Landtag, or Upper House, its function little more than to approve expenditure of government funds. Reaction had again triumphed, as in the rest of Germany, sending thousands of liberty-loving Germans into exile and across the sea to America.

Metternich had managed to keep his country the dominant power in the Germanic Confederation, although in the late years there was increasing rivalry between Austria and Prussia. The disappearance of Austria's leading statesman coincided with the appearance in Prussia of the brilliant, power-obsessed Junker, Otto von Bismarck, as the most powerful leader since Stein. His unconcealed ambition was to raise the status of his country, so often the victim of more powerful European states. As such, he was the leader who would change a nation's destiny. In 1862 as minister-president he took over direction of the Prussian government, the year after the death of Frederick William, who died childless and insane. Frederick William was succeeded by his brother, the 64-year-old William I, a soldier-king who as a youth had fought against Napoleon and after the 1848 revolution had led Prussian forces into Baden and the Palatinate to re-establish autocracy. Personally William was a frugal, simple-minded man, yet convinced like his brother that Hohenzollerns were kings by the grace of God.

The new king reigned, but Bismarck ruled. In 1864, against the will of the Landtag, Bismarck persuaded the Austrians to join with the

Prussians in making war on Denmark with the promise that they should divide and occupy Schleswig-Holstein, a Germanic region the Danes had attempted to annex. Denmark was of course no match for the Austro-Prussian armies, but after the war Bismarck adroitly maneuvered to keep possession of both duchies. The occupation of Schleswig-Holstein was the last cooperative gesture between Austria and Prussia. Within two years their differences had become so acute that both countries were preparing to mobilize. Bismarck welcomed such a conflict. For him the humiliation of Austria was a necessary step to the aggrandizement of Prussia. To his great satisfaction their growing hostility resulted in the Seven Weeks' War, which Austria expected to win and which—to the world's surprise—the Austrians lost overwhelmingly at Sadowa, where more troops met in conflict than had fought two generations earlier at Leipzig. But the Austrian army was bungling, whereas the highly trained Prussians under Count Helmuth von Moltke had absorbed the lessons of the American Civil War, that first modern conflict. In his astonishing victory Moltke gave Europe a surprise demonstration of the Industrial Revolution's military potential by using railroads and telegraph, machine-tooled cannon, breech-loading rifles, and other innovations. "Prussia," the awed London *Spectator* commented after Sadowa, "had leaped in a moment into the position of the first power in Europe."

Bismarck wanted no territory from defeated Austria, being content to destroy the old confederation and eliminate Austria from German affairs. To replace the old, he formed a Prussian-dominated North German Confederation together with the kingdom of Saxony and such smaller states as Oldenburg and Weimar, the whole presided over by himself as Prussian prime minister now raised in rank to imperial chancellor. Although the South German states of Bavaria, Württemberg, Baden, and Hesse-Darmstadt remained outside the new confederation, they nevertheless formed a customs union with it and secretly agreed to place their armies under Prussian control in case of war.

France had maintained its position as Europe's first power by astutely encouraging Austrian and Prussian rivalry. With Austria defeated, Prussia loomed as an ominous, growing threat to the France of the ailing and politically rickety Napoleon III, whose ministers were now eager to recoup sagging fortunes by a preventive war. Bismarck was equally eager for a showdown with France as a means of pushing German unification, convinced as he was that the modern and efficient Prussian war machine could quickly overcome the shoddily organized, poorly led French forces. War hung in the balance after the Cortes in Madrid had offered the vacant Spanish throne to the Catholic Hohenzollern prince Leopold of the minor Swabian Hohenzollern-Sigmaringen line. Rather than face this double Hohenzollern confrontation, the French were prepared to fight. But to Bismarck's bitter disappointment, King William was not, and ordered Prince Leopold to refuse the crown. French insistence, however, that William promise on behalf of his family never to accept any such offer in the future was more than he could agree to. His telegram of explanation to Bismarck from Bad Ems was altered in transit by Bismarck to sound a note of uncompromising belligerency toward the French and was then released for publication. That famous Ems dispatch, in a day when powers still waged war over "national honor," brought on the Franco-Prussian War. Napoleon III signed the war declaration with trembling hand. William was equally dismayed. Bismarck was triumphant.

The war that followed was what the Germans call a "fresh-happy war," over in less than seven weeks. Fought on French soil by three invading German armies, after several costly battles it culminated in the defeat of the French army and the surrender of Napoleon.

Germans were never more enthusiastically conscious of their Germanness, never more anxious for unity than after this great victory. Sedan made the empire inevitable. Every German town and city would bear its Sedanstrasse. Bismarck now deftly remodeled the constitution of the North German Confederation to take in the other German states; the kingdoms of Bavaria, Saxony, and Württemberg; five grand duchies; thirteen duchies and principalities; and the free cities of Hamburg, Bremen, and Lübeck. Alsace-Lorraine was forthrightly annexed.

The victory of Sedan took place on September 1, 1870. Resistance by the forces of the French Republic, which had replaced Napoleon's empire, caused some delay. But after the siege and occupation of Paris, on January 18, 1871, in Versailles's glittering Hall of Mirrors, the reluctant King William, amidst cheers and flashing swords, was proclaimed emperor of the Second German Empire.

CHAPTER XI

THE KAISERS' SECOND EMPIRE

For the two decades after the Franco-Prussian War, Bismarck, the Iron Chancellor and Europe's foremost statesman, would direct the destinies of the Germany he had brought into being. In Germany even more than in the rest of Europe it was the great period of industrialization and the growth of cities, the age of railroads and banking and industrial capitalism and speculative wealth. German industry, from its beginnings in the forties and fifties, took a sharp leap forward. Mining, machinery, textiles, chemistry, and the new electrical industry expanded so rapidly that by the end of the seventies the new Germany had become the first-ranking industrial power on the Continent and several decades later would surpass even England, where the Industrial Revolution had begun. Young Karl Marx described the inevitable expansion and the equally inevitable concentration of wealth and power, but his theory of the increasing misery of the masses was not borne out by the German facts. The new rich were apparent in all their blatancy; the East Elbian Junkers, thanks to the paternal solicitude of the Junker chancellor, thrived on agricultural tariffs; but workmen and white-collar workers also enjoyed their share of the increasing prosperity.

A timeless view of a German farmyard provides the background for Dürer's engraving of the parable of the Prodigal Son.

Bismarck considered the Prussian king and the Junker-dominated social structure of Prussia as part of the divine order of things. Yet the old autocrat was supple enough to bend to the winds of change even when he did not understand them. He thought little of political parties and insisted that he held his office and authority not from the Reichstag but the Kaiser, as the emperor was now styled. Nevertheless he needed a parliamentary majority to pass budgets and laws. At first he worked with the National Liberals, the free-enterprise constitutional party, but did not hesitate to shift to the predominantly Prussian Conservatives, manipulating both parties to his ends. The Catholic Center Party, drawing its strength from outside Prussia, he distrusted; the fourth large party, the Social Democrats, he saw as his real enemy.

Bismarck's differences with the Catholics brought him into years of conflict with the Roman Church, a "culture battle" in which at one point most of the Prussian bishops were in prison or living abroad and thousands of parishes lacked priests. Pius IX's promulgation of the doctrine of papal infallibility was for the German chancellor a challenge to the authority of the state, whose right it was, he maintained, to control the education of priests, regulate their appointments, and restrict their nonclerical activities. He expelled the Jesuits and made civil marriage compulsory, then abolished all religious orders. Pius appealed to Kaiser William. Bismarck retorted that he would not "go to Canossa," recalling Henry IV's submission to the papacy. Nevertheless, in the end he did just that, for he found in his new alliance with the Conservatives that he needed the votes of the Center for his economic and financial plans, needed the Center the more because of the war he was preparing against the Social Democrats.

The Social Democrats made up the one party that disavowed the Bismarckian Empire. As socialists they looked forward to an age of common ownership; as equally sincere democrats they made practical demands for universal suffrage, an eight-hour day, freedom for the trade unions, a progressive income tax, a militia instead of a standing army, all obtained through the democratic process. Bismarck considered them the enemies of the state. Two attempts on the emperor's life in 1878 by radicals furnished him with the pretext—although the Social Democrats were in no way implicated—for forcing his anti-socialist law through the Reichstag. That law, in its way as Draconian as the Carlsbad Decrees, regulated public meetings and the printing and sale of books, and forbade the collection of funds which "by means of social democratic, socialistic, or communistic designs, aim at the overthrow of the existing order of state or society." Social Democratic leaders were jailed or driven into exile. Yet the party grew. In the first Reichstag, in 1871, there had been one socialist deputy. In the 1878 election the party garnered almost half a million votes, a figure tripled a dozen years later when for all Bismarck's efforts thirty-five socialist deputies were elected to the Reichstag. The chancellor attempted to steal the Social Democratic fire by sponsoring his own social measures, such as the Employers' Liability Act. However little gratitude the Social Democrats may have evinced toward their old enemy, Germany became nevertheless through Bismarck the first nation in Europe to adopt such workers' protective measures as compulsory insurance for accidents, sickness, disablement, and old age.

Bismarck achieved his stature as a European statesman in his handling of foreign affairs. Deliberately he had guided his country into three wars as a means, in his own words, of uniting the German "tribes." The ensuing empire he regarded as a "saturated state." He wanted no new territories and displayed marked disinterest in the Volksdeutsch—the Germans living in Austria or the Sudetenland or the Baltic. Only belatedly and reluctantly did he yield to the clamor for colonial acquisitions. What he wished for and what he managed to achieve was peace at home and abroad. He had not even wanted Alsace and Lorraine, but felt obliged to yield to the nationalistic enthusiasm of 1870. For the French the two lost provinces—although Alsace might well have been considered German—became a symbol of national humiliation.

The Iron Chancellor wove a web of alliances, intricate and requiring constant mending, but he gave Germany more than a generation of peace. Most of all he feared enemies hemming in his country on both sides. Since France was bound to nurse dreams of revenge, friendship with Russia remained fundamental for him. Whenever relations became strained between the two countries, he smoothed them over. He signed a defensive treaty with an Austria-Hungary that was this time the junior partner. With his League of the Three Emperors (Russia, Austria, and Germany) he revived the old Holy Alliance. The efforts of the Balkan Slavs, with Russian backing, to shake off Turkish rule brought Austria and Russia into conflict. When war broke out between Russia and Turkey in 1877 over Bulgaria, and Austria showed itself anxious to take its own Balkan areas, Bismarck played the role of the pacifier, the honest broker, remarking with a wisdom that would seem prophetic four decades later that Bulgaria was "not sufficiently important to plunge Europe, from Moscow to the Pyrenees and from the North Sea to Palermo, into a war the outcome of which nobody can foresee; after the war people would not even remember why they had fought." As president of the Berlin Congress of 1878 he worked out a compromise acceptable to Russia, Turkey, and Austria. Above all he kept the peace. He made a tripartite agreement with Italy and Austria in an effort to damp Austrian and Italian enmity. At the same time he signed a secret Reinsurance Treaty with Russia. He spoke pacific words to France and would if he could have signed an alliance with England.

Kaiser William remained in the background. The hated "grape-shot prince," who in 1848 had ordered troops to fire on the Berlin crowd and had been forced to flee the country, had in his old age become a revered father figure. Liberals hoped for and expected much from Crown Prince Frederick William, a constitutionalist, a believer in parliamentary democracy, married to an opinionated and energetic daughter of Queen Victoria. The old Kaiser died in 1888 in his ninety-first year. By the time Frederick William came to the throne at the age of fifty-six as Frederick III, he already had an advanced cancer of the larynx. He reigned, if one can consider a dying man as reigning, a mere ninety-nine days.

Following in the family tradition of Hohenzollern enmity, Frederick's son, the thirty-year-old Prince Frederick William, who would become Kaiser William II, despised his father and hated his mother. However well the young William managed to conceal it, he was a cripple, having suffered birth injuries that left him with an impaired sense of balance and a withered left arm. Psychically he was even more crippled, both by his injury and the sternness of his upbringing, and he compensated as Kaiser by blatant military posturings which were in fact no more than those of an actor strutting on the stage. A man of good intentions, quick intelligence, bad taste, and a shallow mind, he was incapable of intellectual concentration. If life had been a constant

military pageant, he would have been a happy ruler, leading his guards triumphantly on maneuvers, changing from one uniform to the other. He did his best to make his dream come true. In the first seventeen years of his reign he redesigned his officers' uniforms thirty-seven times. Yet war, actual war, frightened him, for all the jingoistic intemperance of the speeches he so loved to give. Beneath his seeming energy and bustle he was lazy, pleasure-loving, occupying himself chiefly by traveling with aimless haste from city to city of his realm to show himself to applauding crowds. Where his grandfather had thought of himself as king of Prussia, saddled with an imperial crown, the grandson thought of himself first as German emperor. As a Hohenzollern he felt responsible to no one but God. For all his love of uniforms and parades, he knew next to nothing of real soldiering. His thirty-year reign gave its name to the Wilhelmian style—resembling the Victorian in England and that of the Gilded Age in the United States—pompous, overornamented, massive, a profligacy of plush and gilt. His court had its decorators and painters and even poets, but the real culture of the period developed beyond his ken. He liked to boast

Casting operations at the great Krupp foundry, located in the Ruhr Valley coal and iron district, as painted by Otto Bollhagen in 1873

that the will of the Kaiser was the supreme law, but he himself had no real will. His glossy gravity-defying mustache, such as Frederick William's giant grenadiers had once worn, became almost his trademark, and he was so proud of the mustache stiffener he had invented to keep the ends pointed skyward that he had it patented under the trade name "Es Ist Erreicht" (It Is Attained). In the end, with the best of intentions, this shallow, vain, well-meaning man would destroy his house.

The Wilhelmian era was one of expansive prosperity for a Germany rapidly transforming itself from the loose Prussian-led federation of 1870 to a powerful, concentrated nation-state. Yet the dichotomy between Prussia and the rest of Germany remained. The Prussian Landtag, with a limited elective system weighted heavily in favor of property, remained unshakably conservative. The Reichstag, elected by universal franchise, by comparison was more liberal or "leftish." Over the decades the strength of the Social Democrats, regarded with as much hostility by William as by Bismarck, grew to a million and a half votes and formed the largest block of deputies in the Reichstag.

Germany, florid and prosperous, was the new-rich nation of Europe, with all the *arriviste* confidence of wealth and the arrogance bred of insecurity. Bourgeois German hearts beat faster at the sight of their parvenu, saber-rattling Kaiser. The satirical weekly, *Simplicissimus,* might poke fun at the multiuniformed emperor—always with the risk of a jail term for the editor—but most solid householders had a framed picture of the imperial family on the wall. The army, that symbol of symbols, in which each able-bodied man served three years, grew in size as it did in the awed esteem of the German people. But Bismarck's "saturated state" no longer satisfied the expansionists who found their outlet in the Pan-German Union and the Navy League, the latter supported by the Kaiser and Admiral Alfred von Tirpitz, who vociferously demanded a navy second to none. Through the dull decades of peace, young German officers in their messes drank to "the Day."

Inevitably there would be a collision between the young emperor of the absolutist Hohenzollern tradition and the old chancellor who had been the real ruler of the new empire since its inception. The collision that led to Bismarck's resignation was over labor law reform, but the issue itself was irrelevant. By the time William came to the throne, the empire's epic years were over. Bismarck had run his course, and even a wiser monarch might have followed the Kaiser's flighty example in forcing the old chancellor's resignation. In the few years left to Bismarck he would become a legend, with Bismarck towers springing up all over Germany, and every city with a Bismarck street or place. Yet at the time of the Iron Chancellor's resignation he could by no means have been considered a popular figure.

Most of the thirty years of William's reign encompassed a rising, confident prosperity. Even the Social Democrats, though William continued to regard them as aliens, drifted from their earlier recalcitrant Marxism to a gradual and ameliorative democratic socialism. Nor for all their exclusion and their hostility to the Kaiser did they feel any less patriotic than the self-satisfied middle classes. Social Democratic leaders like Friedrich Ebert and Gustav Noske aimed more for a welfare state than for any social overturn. Noske, in fact, boasted that he had never read Marx and never intended to.

Externally William's reign was marked by Germany's increasing political isolation and by recurrent war crises. As the age moved into the new century, during those years that in the disastrous aftertime would be regarded as "the good old days," war seemed to most Europeans both impossible and inevitable.

The four chancellors—Caprivi, Hohenlohe, Bülow, and Bethmann-Hollweg—who followed in Bismarck's heavy steps, would each in turn find it impossible to work with the impulsive and unpredictable Kaiser. Under Caprivi the Russian Reinsurance Treaty was allowed to lapse, a dereliction for which William has been much blamed. Yet the emergence of Germany as the strongest industrial and military power in Europe made the *rapprochement* of republican France and czarist Russia an inevitable protective measure which even the Iron Chancellor's deft diplomacy would have been powerless to prevent.

At the century's turn the British in their isolation felt the need of looking for potential allies. Since French and British interests had clashed in Africa, and since Russia was the old enemy in the Near and Far East, Germany, having no basic conflict with England, seemed to offer the most suitable alliance. The Kaiser and his chancellor let this great opportunity slip past them. A durable Anglo-German alliance would have been possible only if Germany had been willing to forego its naval construction program. This the Kaiser, out of dreams of empire, and Admiral Tirpitz, on strategic grounds, refused to consider. "The Royal Navy is a dire necessity, the German fleet a luxury," the young Winston Churchill pointed out in 1912. The Kaiser on the other hand insisted that he could not and would not "allow John Bull to dictate to me the speed of my ship-building." This and the growing rivalry in industry, trade, and shipping turned the British to seeking an agreement with the French in 1904 and with Russia three years later. As the German historian Golo Mann, son of Thomas Mann, wrote: "Frightened by the growth of the German navy, shocked by the Kaiser's boasts and the subversive activities of the Pan-Germans, incited by the lies and panicking of its yellow press, Britain gradually slipped into the Franco-Russian camp."

Germany and Austria, in the dubious and unreliable company of Italy, found themselves boxed in by the triple alliance of France, Russia, and England. War signs, like heat lightning, continued to flicker on the darkening international horizon, but at each recurring crisis war itself was averted. French dominance in Morocco brought on the Crisis of 1905, when Germany demanded protection for its own economic interests in North Africa. Baron von Holstein, the gray eminence of the German Foreign Office, hoping to isolate France and break up the Anglo-French alliance, even advocated a preventive war. An understanding among the powers was reached at a general conference held in Algeciras in southern Spain which gave at least lip service to the principle of equality of commercial and economic interests in Morocco, but which also paved the way for secret war agreements between England and France. Not only was the lightning seen but the thunder reverberated in the Agadir Crisis of 1911. Since the sultan of Morocco was unable to protect foreign interests, the French had disregarded the Algeciras settlement by setting out to make that North African region their own. Pan-Germans, protesting German exclusion, now demanded western Morocco as compensation. Then in July the German gunboat *Panther* steamed into the Moroccan port of Agadir, ostensibly to protect German lives and property but actually as a warning. The German ambassador to France then expressed willingness to abandon his country's Moroccan claims in exchange for the French Congo, and though this at first set off war alarms, German and French negotiators managed to work out a settlement by which Germany received a portion of the Congo, and France, far more importantly, was allowed to impose a protectorate over Morocco.

Further crises followed within the ethnic turbulence of the Balkans and the disintegrating Turkish Empire. Two Balkan wars occurred, in 1912 and 1913, in the first of which Bulgaria, Serbia, and Greece all but expelled the Turks from Europe. Fearful of pan-Slavic expansion, Austria-Hungary resisted Serbia's successful push to the Adriatic, while Russia backed its fellow Slavs. General war came close, as Austria-Hungary and Russia both mobilized, but Great Britain and Germany this time united in forcing a peaceful settlement. The second Balkan war, a quarrel of the Balkan victors over the spoils, lasted only a month and resulted in the doubling in size of Austria-Hungary's minor but ruthless Slavic enemy, Serbia.

Each ensuing crisis was like a wave that surged farther and farther up the beach until at the last moment it receded. But the haunting fear was of the one wave that would not recede, that would finally engulf the shore line. So the year 1914 dawned, that year fated to destroy dynasties, alter the map of Europe, change the face of the world, and usher in the age of violence that is still with us. President Wilson's personal envoy, Colonel Edward House, described the European situation as "militarism run stark mad." On June 28, the nephew and heir of the Austrian emperor Francis Joseph, Archduke Francis Ferdinand, together with his morganatic wife, was assassinated while riding through the streets of the Bosnian capital of Sarajevo. The shots were fired by the young Serbian student Gavrilo Princip, but the assassination plot was the work of the Pan-Slavic Black Hand Society, whose agents had been trained and equipped in Serbia and whose intentions were known to the Serbian government.

During the fateful month of July, as the last wave gathered strength, a Bismarck might still have avoided the coming war. But there were no such leaders; only a senile emperor who had reigned as long as anyone could remember, a thin-minded, stubborn czar, and a Kaiser under the illusion that he was both a peerless diplomat and a great military captain; only foreign ministers who were weak or vain or confused. With much justification the Austrians held the Serbian government responsible for the assassinations. Austria's subsequent ultimatum to Serbia was, however, intended to bring on a localized war that would put down Serbian Pan-Slavism for good. Serbia met most but not all the Austrian demands. The Kaiser encouraged Austrian intransigence, even as the Russians announced their solidarity with their Serbian brothers, and republican France prepared to go to the aid of its czarist ally. Exactly one month after the murders at Sarajevo, Austria declared war on Serbia. Whereupon the alarmed Czar Nicholas was reluctantly persuaded to mobilize and an equally alarmed Kaiser and chancellor in Berlin now urged moderation on Austria. Events were beyond them. The irreversible, fateful machinery of war had been set in motion. Germany sent an ultimatum to Russia to cease war preparations, then mobilized in turn, as did the French. At the last minute the British proposed a conference, then asked for direct negotiations between Vienna and Saint Petersburg. It was too late. No reply came from the czar as his armies gathered. On August 1, Germany declared war on Russia and two days later on France. The armies were on the move. Germany's thrust across Belgium, in violation of a treaty signed in 1839, would have been tolerated by the Belgian king Albert except for the fiery opposition of the Socialist Party leader Vandervelde. Belgium's resistance and Bethmann-Hollweg's unfortunate if accurate description of the century-old treaty as "a scrap of paper" gave England's foreign secretary, Sir Edward Grey, the open excuse he needed beyond his secret commitments to bring his country to the side of France in the engulfing struggle. Italy prudently chose temporary neutrality.

Historians would argue for the next generation over who and what country was responsible for the First World War and never find agreement. What could not be argued or denied however was the wave of enthusiasm that swept over the nations at the war's outbreak. Suddenly, and all too briefly, brotherliness transcended class and regional antagonism, uniting people in a common cause for which they would gladly offer up their lives. Even the extreme-left Social Democrats in the Reichstag voted for war. Crowds gathered in Berlin to march with impromptu gaiety down the great boulevard Unter den Linden, cheering, waving flags, singing patriotic songs. Similar crowds, gripped by the heady contagion of patriotism, filled the streets of Moscow and Saint Petersburg, as did other crowds in Paris. In London a vast throng gathered before Buckingham Palace to call the small bearded man, their king, to the balcony as they sang the national anthem. "Now God be thanked Who has matched us with His Hour," Rupert Brooke wrote in the exuberance of this ephemeral mood.

It was a mood the rulers and statesmen did not share. England's foreign secretary, Lord Grey, saw the lamps of Europe going out one by one and knew they would not be lighted again in his lifetime. Ex-Chancellor Bülow happened to meet the Kaiser just after the war declaration and found him with Bethmann-Hollweg looking "pallid, frightened. . . almost desperate." Bülow asked Hollweg, "incredibly helpless and sad," how on earth it had all happened. "Heaven knows," the chancellor said, raising his arms in a hopeless gesture.

The Kaiser had had one look into the abyss, but then he averted his eyes. Bidding his troops Godspeed, he promised them that they would return before the leaves fell. The German plan of battle was one developed a decade earlier by the chief of staff, Count Alfred von Schlieffen, in which seven eighths of the German army would make an enveloping sweep through Belgium behind France's border defenses and then in one climactic battle defeat the French and occupy Paris. It would be another Sedan; all over in six weeks. The remaining fraction of the army stationed in the East would hold off the Russians until after their comrades' victory in the West. Then the whole weight of Germany would be thrown against Russia in a campaign that was certain to end before leaf-fall.

Whether Schlieffen, if he had been commander, could have carried out his plan before the leaves fell remains a military academic question. The commanding German general, Helmuth von Moltke, a nephew of the 1870 Moltke, was no Schlieffen but an elderly, ailing man with an unmilitary interest in Christian Science and the philosophy of Rudolf Steiner. In his uncertain hands Schlieffen's plan fell apart. When the Kaiser, in nervous terror of a Russian invasion of East Prussia, demanded that two additional army corps be sent there, Moltke sent them from the West, where they might have swung the balance. At the Marne River ninety miles east of Paris, the German and French armies finally met, the French being reinforced by Sir John French's British Expeditionary Force. The Battle of the Marne, in which the Germans were thrown back and their myth of invincibility shattered, was one of the most important if not the most important of the century. A German repulse there, however little the participants realized it, meant that this would be no "fresh-happy" six weeks' war but one that would go on over the years to become the greatest, the costliest, the bloodiest that the world had yet known, fought more bitterly because it was fought for no comprehensible reason. For the next four years the battle lines would remain static in the West, while the armies of the Allies and Germany crouched behind trenches strung four hundred miles from the North Sea to Switzerland and only a few hundred yards apart. Misconceived offensives would result in trivial and temporary gains of territory and enormous casualties. Winters would follow summers as men endured the mass slaughters of the Somme and Verdun, and a generation died. "What of the faith and fire within us?" the aged Thomas Hardy had written of the men he saw marching away in 1914. Faith and fire both were extinguished in the trenches. Other nations were sucked into the maelstrom: Turkey and Bulgaria on the side of Germany and Austria; Italy, Rumania, Greece, and finally in the faith-and-fire mood of 1914 an ingenuous United States on the side of the Allies, as well as peripherally Japan, China, Liberia, and a dozen South American countries.

Germany's defeat of Russia, and the revolution there, released German reinforcements for the West but brought no change where defense had shown itself so superior to offense. Blockaded by the British Navy, Germany was slowly starving. Long before the war William II seemed little more than an emblazoned figurehead. As the war progressed he became a cipher, inconsequent among the military, disregarded as a political figure, valued only by the Allies as the villain of the piece. Chancellors, succeeding Bethmann-Hollweg, were nebulous figures. As the war went on, the bull-necked quartermaster general Erich Ludendorff became the real ruler of Germany. He was an extraordinary organizer and planner, crude and cruel, and an arrogant believer in total war. Until the war's end he held the reins of power behind the massive shadow of the old and, by now, semilegendary Hindenburg. Yet even as Ludendorff assumed control, even as Germans hungered and died amidst the usual profiteers and new-rich, the war was becoming a people's war. Those who fought, those who hungered, those who endured, would have their say when it was over. That was clear even to Admiral Tirpitz, who admitted that "the existing caste and class system is finished. Victory or defeat, we shall have pure

A trip on the Rhine was almost obligatory for Victorian travelers. Tidy towns and ruined castles (like these at Kaub) passed in picturesque succession.

democracy." In 1917 in the Reichstag the parties of the Center, the left-wing Liberals, and the Social Democrats—now a majority—passed a peace resolution. Ludendorff was indeed dictator, but the voice of parliamentary democracy was growing stronger.

The torpedoing of the munitions-laden British passenger ship *Lusitania* in 1915 had, however illogically, hardened American opinion against Germany. Resumption of unrestricted submarine warfare in 1917 in a desperate German effort to break the stranglehold of the British blockade inevitably brought the United States into the war. In one final effort in the spring of 1918, Ludendorff gathered all his reserves for the "Michael" Offensive, the last great German drive. The Allies fell back, and for some weeks the Michael Offensive seemed to tremble on the verge of success. In the end the Germans lacked the strength, the resources to carry it through. When the French and the British, with the help of fresh American forces, brought the offensive to a halt, Ludendorff knew that the war was lost. The Allied counteroffensive, launched on August 8, rolled over the defensive Hindenburg Line, shattering the German Army. "The blackest day in the history of Germany," Ludendorff called it.

President Wilson's Fourteen Points, which seemed a life raft to the Social Democrats and the Centrists, hastened the German disintegration. Even as the army spent its last strength in vain, the home front was on its way to collapsing. Ludendorff, his nerves gone, warned the politicians in Berlin of a total collapse if there was not an immediate armistice. On September 29 the Kaiser found himself forced to sign a decree granting a parliamentary government on British lines. A peace cabinet of Centrists, Progressives, and Social Democrats was formed under the Liberal Prince Max of Baden, a wise and sober realist who insisted on Ludendorff's dismissal and who—together with the Austrian foreign minister—appealed to Wilson for an armistice on the basis of the Fourteen Points. The left-wing Social Democrats, under Karl Liebknecht, had broken away to form the Spartacus League, nucleus of Germany's future Communist Party.

As autumn moved toward winter a naval mutiny broke out in Kiel and spread to other parts and to the army. Soldiers' and sailors' councils formed. Red flags appeared in Munich, Hamburg, Bremen, Cologne, and other cities. In Berlin mobs gathered in the streets. From the insecurity of his capital the Kaiser left for the security of his military headquarters in Spa, Belgium. Vainly, Prince Max urged him to abdicate. In an exchange of notes prefatory to an armistice, the star-crossed professor who was President of the United States announced primly that he would not negotiate if he had to deal with "the military masters and the monarchical autocrats of Germany." The note was the knell of the house of Hohenzollern. Possibly the Kaiser might have preserved the dynasty if he had abdicated earlier, but he still clung to the increasingly absurd idea that he was needed and wanted, that his soldiers were loyal to him. It took Hindenburg and General Groener finally to disabuse him of this notion. The home troops were mutinous, they told him. The army in the field would follow its captains. It would no longer follow the discredited emperor.

The Social Democratic leader Ebert, a pragmatic socialist and loyal democrat, wanted a constitutional monarchy with a regency acting in the name of the Kaiser's grandson. But in Berlin a revolutionary situation threatened. Liebknecht with his doctrinaire intransigence was prepared to proclaim a German Soviet Republic on Lenin's model. To forestall him, and mindful of Wilson, Socialist leader Philipp Scheidemann from the great staircase of the Reichstag library proclaimed to a throng below: "Long live the great German Republic!" Hindenburg and Groener now warned the Kaiser that if he remained anywhere in Germany he ran the risk of being brought back to Berlin by revolutionary soldiers, that he had no choice but exile.

Early on the morning of November 10, the day before the armistice, the Kaiser arrived at the closed Dutch frontier. All day he waited at the Eisjden railway station for permission to cross the border, striding up and down the platform, chain-smoking cigarettes and talking compulsively at random. Not until late in the afternoon did the news finally come that the Dutch would grant him asylum.

1522

CHAPTER XII

THE WEIMAR REPUBLIC BANKRUPTED

Prince Max of Baden, the last imperial chancellor, and Friedrich Ebert, the first republican chancellor-to-be, met in the Berlin chancellery on November 11, 1919. "Herr Ebert," said Prince Max in the chancellery to his successor, the leader of the Social Democrats, "I commit the German Empire to your keeping." "I have lost two sons for this Empire," Ebert answered quietly as he took over the government. The pudgy 47-year-old ex-saddler and his party had come to power reluctantly, as receivers in bankruptcy for a hungry and broken nation where power had almost ceased to exist. The Pan-Germans, the monarchists, the nationalists, had suddenly become invisible. In Berlin, Liebknecht and his Spartacists had seized control of a number of public buildings. Workers' and Soldiers' Councils sprang up almost spontaneously. Armed soldiers drove about in trucks, flying red flags, while revolutionary civilians shouldered rifles that they had bought or taken from more timid soldiers. The new chancellor had at least a few straws of hope in the fact that Hindenburg and Groener, speaking for what was left of the High Command, had agreed to support the government in maintaining order and in the "fight against Bolshevism."

The spiritual anguish and physical suffering of Germany in the 1920s and 1930s are anticipated in Dürer's etching "The Man of Sorrows."

 To the generals was given the well-nigh impossible task of bringing back an army of two million men in thirty-one days from France, Belgium, Luxemburg, the German Rhineland, and Alsace-Lorraine. It was the kind of coordinated miracle of which the German general staff was capable. The troops marched back in order under their officers, sometimes even with flags flying and bands playing. But no sooner had they crossed their own borders than they became an uncoordinated mass of field-gray civilians concerned chiefly with getting to their homes as quickly as possible. When the High Command dispatched nine divisions to Berlin to disarm the population and restore order, the ranks on arriving simply dissolved. In the capital control lapsed. Soldiers wearing red badges tore the epaulets from officers they met on the street. Liebknecht continued to inflame the mobs with incandescent oratory. The new chancellor lived in mortal danger.

Under Ebert's direction a six-man Council of People's Commissioners replaced the imperial cabinet. With the Social Democratic leader as chairman, the council was divided equally between the Majority Socialists and the Independents. At first the council issued a spate of decrees, enacting an eight-hour day, abolishing censorship, releasing political prisoners, increasing sickness, old-age, and unemployment benefits, and giving labor the unrestricted right to organize. Then the wheels seemed to run down, neither faction trusting the other. No effort was made to summon the old Reichstag that had been elected in 1912. To the right of the Socialists, the Conservatives and even the Catholic Center seemed to have collapsed. Meanwhile on the far left Liebknecht, out of the drifters and adventurers he found on the streets, began forming a Council of Deserters, Stragglers, and Furloughed Soldiers, shock troops of revolution. The People's Naval Division, made up of red ex-sailors, occupied parts of the imperial palace. There were Spartacist riots in Munich, Hamburg, Halle, Düsseldorf, Dortmund, and Schwerin. Germany itself seemed on the point of dissolving into its pre-Bismarckian fragments. In Munich the bohemian-radical intellectual, Kurt Eisner, had seized power and proclaimed a "Bavarian Republic." Liebknecht now transformed his Spartacus League into the Communist Party of Germany and prepared a putsch in Berlin.

Ebert's hope was to be able to hang on until the third week in January, when there would be a general election for a constitutional assembly. But by New Year's Day, 1919, it seemed doubtful that the casually proclaimed republic could survive that long. Germany was starving. Because of bickering among the Allies, the blockade still continued. The unemployed, demobilized soldiers and refugees crowded by thousands into the cities. Yet even as Liebknecht plotted his German sequel to Russia's October Revolution, a countermovement was underway. Ebert had appointed as minister of defense the ruthless and energetic Gustav Noske, an ex-basketweaver enamored of the military and utterly opposed to the Spartacists. The High Command pledged Noske its unqualified support. Meanwhile, outside Berlin various higher officers were organizing that minority of tough veteran soldiers who did not want to be demobilized, who considered themselves professionals, preferred army life and took a grim pleasure in fighting. These soldiers of fortune were now enlisted into well-equipped, well-disciplined units called Free Corps.

On January 6 the anticipated Spartacist revolt broke out, Liebknecht's force being joined by the Independent Socialists and the revolutionary Shop Stewards. At first the revolutionaries carried everything before them, occupying most of the government buildings, even placing sharpshooters on top of the Brandenburg Gate. The disheartened Ebert remained barricaded in his chancellery. Noske fled the city. From Russia Lenin expressed his delight at the radical turn of events. Liebknecht's street fighters, confident of the support of the Berlin workers and unaware of the military forces gathering against them, expected little concerted opposition. Suddenly the field-gray columns of the Free Corps marched into the city, led by Noske; soldiers trained in street fighting, equipped with machine guns, howitzers, armored cars, and tanks. At once they deployed, with rapid and brutal proficiency breaking up the Spartacist ranks. Liebknecht was captured by Free Corps soldiers, beaten, and shot, as was the famous woman Spartacist leader Rosa Luxemburg, who had actually been opposed to the revolt. In a week it was all over and the provisional government, backed by Free Corps bayonets, was in complete control.

The general election held a few days after the Spartacists had been put down was a triumph of moderation. Thirty of the 35 million eligible Germans voted. On the left the Independents—the Communists having boycotted the election—received a mere 7 per cent of the

vote. On the right the two monarchical parties, the Conservatives, who now styled themselves the German National People's Party, and the German People's Party (the old National Liberals), received 15 per cent. The German Democratic Party (once the Progressives) also won 18 per cent, while the Center bettered that by two points. With 39 per cent of the votes and 163 of the 423 seats, the Social Democrats became the largest party in the assembly, but without an absolute majority their leaders were unable to embark on a program of nationalization.

The National Assembly was convened to appoint a permanent government, make peace with the Allies, and draft a new constitution. Weimar, the city of Goethe and Schiller, was the site chosen as a symbol of German humanistic culture in opposition to the authoritarianism and militarism of Prussia. That constitution of high ideals and good intentions attempted to revive the dream of 1848, even adopting the black-red-gold flag of seven decades earlier. But the enthusiastic optimism of 1848 bore little resemblance to the pessimistic mood of 1918 and 1919. Weimar's constitution assumed that all Germans would adjust their differences within its liberal framework. On paper the constitution looked democratically impressive; universal suffrage for citi-

German Expressionist Max Beckmann attacked what he viewed as the corruptness of contemporary life in satirical works like "Family Picture," 1926.

zens over twenty; direct election of a president who would appoint a chancellor and cabinet responsive to the Reichstag; a Reichstag itself elected by proportional representation; federal states under the control of the central government; private property subordinate to public welfare; freedom of labor to organize, and so on. In extraordinary emergencies, the president through Article 48 would rule by emergency decrees. Yet the structure was built on sand. The republic had inherited by default a defeated empire stripped of a tenth of its population, an eighth of its territory, much of its coal resources, and most of its iron. Officials of the Kaiser's time remained in office, as did professors, teachers, and judges, men loyal to the old order rather than the new. Noske and Ebert had had to turn to monarchist generals for support, given, they would discover, without any underlying allegiance.

Even before the new constitution had been completed for submission to the voters, the Assembly was forced to face up to the Treaty of Versailles. Wilson had led the Germans to expect a peace of reconciliation on the basis of his Fourteen Points. Instead they now found themselves confronted with a peace of revenge, dictated chiefly by France. Germany was required to admit herself to be the "sole and only author of the war" and to agree to pay reparations of an undefined amount sufficient to redeem all the Allied costs. Germans designated as war criminals were to be turned over to the Allies for judgment. Alsace and Lorraine of course went back to France, and only with difficulty were the French dissuaded from annexing the Rhineland and the Saarland, both of which regions they would now occupy under a fifteen-year mandate. Among other territories lost by Germany were West Prussia and Posen—which went to the revived Poland, with Danzig a free city, and the Polish corridor dividing East Prussia from the rest of Germany as it had in the seventeenth century. Parts of Silesia and Memel were also removed from German suzerainty. The German army was to be limited to 100,000 men, the navy to six battleships, and Germany could have no submarines or warplanes. All German colonies and overseas investments were forfeit. Nor was the wish of dismembered Austria to join with the German Republic to be allowed.

The reparations clauses were intended not only to squeeze Germany dry but to keep the German nation in a permanent state of impotence. Earlier the National Assembly had elected Ebert as first president of the republic and he had appointed Scheidemann the first chancellor. Faced with what the Nationalists and National Socialists came to call the Versailles Dictate, Chancellor Scheidemann resigned, declaring that his hand would wither if he signed. All the delegates except for the Independent Socialists called for the treaty's rejection. But the more realistic High Command informed the Assembly through Groener and Hindenburg that such an act of defiance would lead to an immediate occupation by the Allies in which the name of Germany would vanish from the map. There was no choice, the generals insisted, but capitulation.

Between the meeting of the National Assembly and the Great Depression lay a period of ten maturing years for the Weimar Republic. The first five years would be turbulent, marked by Communist uprisings, political assassinations by the fanatic right, the 1920 *putsch* led by the inept conservative Wolfgang Kapp which was broken by a general strike, the occupation of the industrial Ruhr heartland by the French as a claim on delayed reparations payments, and a complete collapse of the German currency. In 1914 four marks had been worth one American dollar; by the end of 1923 the rate had become 4.2 trillion. The impoverished middle-class citizens, the backbone of the Kaiser's Germany, increasingly lost whatever faith they may have had in the Weimar Republic. "The system," the republic's enemies called it, spreading the legend ever wider that the German army had never been defeated in the field but stabbed in the back by socialist parliamentary traitors. Rabid antisemitic nationalists and Free Corps adventurers carried on their political assassinations with relative immunity. Matthias Erzberger, the Centrist leader who had signed the armistice agreement, was assassinated by Nationalists two and a half years later as was the foreign minister, Walter Rathenau, the brilliant Jewish industrialist and statesman whose organization of the War Raw Materials Department in 1914 had enabled Germany to fight a four-year war. Violence became a way of life. In Bavaria, more separatist even than in the Kaiser's time, a Soviet Republic was overthrown by government forces. Later Ludendorff and an Austrian agitator-fanatic of ferocious oratorical gifts, Adolf Hitler, launched the Munich "Beer Hall Putsch" in an ineffectual though bloody attempt to seize the Bavarian and then the Berlin government under the aegis of a catchall new party called the National Socialist German Workers' (Nazi) Party.

As Ebert well understood, under a constitutional monarchy the Weimar transplant might have struck roots of its own. Those roots never did develop. As after all extended wars, speculators managed to profit by the convulsions of society. Amidst the general decay of the postwar period, a mushroom growth of new-rich sprang up. The archcapitalist Hugo Stinnes manipulated his holdings to make himself the master of the greatest industrial empire the world had ever known, even as the fall of the mark expropriated whole segments of the community. Disillusionment spread. In the first Reichstag elections after the Weimar Assembly, the Social Democrats lost heavily, while the Independent Socialists—now joined by the Communists—gained on the left and the old national parties doubled their strength on the right. The government that ensued was solidly bourgeois. In the frequent cabinet shifts of the Weimar Republic, the Social Democrats would several times join coalition governments, but never again would the party have the strength and influence that it had just after the armistice. France's occupation of the Ruhr, which nearly completed the breakdown of social order, also brought about the emergence of the Weimar Republic's most outstanding political figure, Gustav Stresemann. The 45-year-old Stresemann, a monarchist, had in 1917 been the leader of the future People's Party, the party of big business and finance. In the grim latter months of 1923 he became chancellor of a Grand Coalition, made up of his business party plus the Social Democrats, the Center, and the Democrats. With his square face, small blue eyes, and shaved head, Stresemann looked a caricature German, but he was a man of great energy and character, a brilliant speaker, and even in his early middle age capable of growing with events. As chancellor he became briefly almost a dictator, stabilizing the currency with the new Rentenmark, moving against a Communist threat in Thuringia and Saxony and more hesitantly against the right-wing threat in Bavaria that culminated in the Beer Hall Putsch. With his policy of stabilization and drastic retrenchment, the feverish employment of inflation gave way to deflation, temporary unemployment, and a rising discontent that finally brought down his cabinet. Stresemann stayed on, however, as foreign minister in succeeding cabinets until his death in 1929.

His few months as chancellor had altered the country and altered him. From a German nationalist he had become a European. What he henceforth lived for was to restore Germany to the family of Europe, to make his country once more united, great, and respected. The old national enmities, he felt, must be buried and Germany must for the time accept the penalties of defeat. While chancellor he had been preparing a restudy of the reparations problem. That problem became at least temporarily manageable with the adoption of the Dawes Plan, a conciliatory formula developed by the American financier Charles Dawes, which marked the end of the bloodless economic war between Germany and France. The plan called for the evacuation of the Ruhr, an international loan to Germany, and a scaling down of reparations payments to allow the rebuilding of Germany. From the Dawes Plan, Stresemann led his country to the negotiations with England's Austen Chamberlain and France's Aristide Briand that resulted in the Locarno Pact, in which Germany accepted the western frontiers and the demilitarization of the Rhineland and pledged the settlement of all other disputes by peaceful means. In return Germany was to be admitted to the League of Nations. Locarno was essentially a peace pact, and for their efforts at mutual understanding, Stresemann and Chamberlain and Briand were awarded the Nobel Peace Prize.

As a result of the infusion of foreign loans following the Dawes Plan and the Locarno Pact, Germany acquired the means as well as the will to become one of the most productive countries in the world. In contrast to the overstuffed stability of the Kaiser's time, the Weimar Republic developed a frenetic gaiety, most apparent in the raffish glitter of Berlin. For the German capital rapidly became the most sophisticated, the freest, the most decadent city in Europe. The art and theater world found a brilliant hothouse flowering in Expressionism. The sleek Bauhaus style replaced Wilhelmian baroque. For those without roots but with means, Berlin in the twenties was the city of cities. William L. Shirer, viewing Germany of the later twenties with sympathetic enthusiasm, thought that life seemed more free, more modern, more exciting there than any place he had ever seen. "Nowhere else did the arts or the intellectual life seem so lively. In contemporary writing, painting, architecture, in music and drama there were new currents or fine talents. And everywhere there was an accent on youth."

The mood of confidence and sense of recovery, as production topped the 1914 figure, was reflected in the election returns. Already in the

1924 Reichstag election the delegates from the right extremist bloc, which included the National Socialists, fell from 32 to 14 in a total of 491 seats. The Communists on the left and the fanatics on the right seemed stopped in their tracks. Stresemann's policies even withstood the election of the retired Hindenburg to the presidency in 1925 following the death of Ebert, an election that would not have succeeded if the Communists had not insisted on running their party hack, Ernst Thälmann, in opposition to the Centrist chancellor, Dr. Wilhelm Marx, the candidate of the Social Democrats and the Center. Contrary to monarchist expectations the elderly Hindenburg as president would honor his oath to the republic.

In the Reichstag elections of 1928 Hitler, appealing to the less respectable nationalists, the antisemites, and the flotsam of voters—the drifters, crackpots, and adventurers—was able to elect only a dozen delegates. The Communists won a hard core of 54 delegates, while the Social Democrats, the party most closely identified with the Weimar Republic, polled 9.5 million votes, a gain of 1.27 million from four years earlier, to win 152 Reichstag seats. The 4.3 million votes of the Nationalists, the monarchist, industrialist party, won 78 seats, as opposed to the 103 received in 1924. With Hindenburg to lend a quasi-monarchical stability, the Weimar Republic seemed at last secure.

Two years would destroy the illusion. In October, 1929, Stresemann died. That same month the stock market crash in the United States set off the cataclysm. Even before then the German economy had begun to falter. With the onset of the Great Depression the easy influx of American money ceased. Germany had managed to borrow far more than had been paid back in reparations. Although the Young Plan, which succeeded the Dawes Plan, reduced still further the reparations burden, it made no allowance for the growing economic crisis. The shadow of the Depression spread rapidly over Germany, enveloping trade, agriculture, banking, industry. The unemployed tramped the streets or queued in front of the welfare offices for their weekly dole. From a nuisance sect, National Socialism expanded overnight to a major party. Its shrill-voiced demagogues, led by the clubfooted nihilist Joseph Goebbels, denounced the Versailles Dictate, reparations, the November criminals (referring to those who signed the armistice and established the republic), the Weimar Republic and its multiplicity of political parties, the Communists, the Jews, the System! In every city brown-shirted SA, or Storm Troopers, bellowed their slogans: "Germans Awake!" "Work and Bread"; "Down with the Jews"; and from an eccentric Nationalist who committed suicide in the twenties, they borrowed the conception of a Third Empire, a Third Reich.

From Bavaria the swastika banners of National Socialism advanced across Swabia and Franconia to Thuringia, Hesse, and finally Berlin. As dissension made the Reichstag increasingly unable to govern, Hindenburg fell back on the Constitution's Article 48. He now appointed the chairman of the Center, Heinrich Brüning, as chancellor. Brüning, an austere, cloistered bachelor, much resembling his Jesuit brother, ruled by the presidential emergency decrees. The new chancellor attempted to overcome the crisis through a grim policy of deflation and retrenchment, bringing the budget into line by lowering wages, cutting social services, and regulating and controlling the economy by further arbitrary decrees. But for all his efforts, unemployment increased, until at least one German in four was unemployed. For the young worker starting out in life, for the university student nearing the end of his studies, there was little or no prospect of a job. Increasingly, the dispossessed, above all the young, turned to the strident promises of National Socialism and the magnetism of its dynamic leader. An election was held in July, 1930, and the National Socialists increased their seats from 12 to an astounding 107. Prudent industrialists and businessmen in turn considered it a kind of insurance to contribute to the Hitler movement. What the government could not offer, the movement did. Men drifting in aimless indigence suddenly achieved a purpose by joining the Brown Shirts. Instead of rejection they found acceptance, in a way of life that offered them a uniform, meals, pocket-money, a sense of solidarity, and the emotional release of violence. Night after night in the great cities of Germany the Brown Shirts and the Red Front Fighters battled for the streets. University students grew overwhelmingly and defiantly National Socialistic, ready to riot and drive anti-Nazi or non-Aryan professors from the podium.

Two obstacles blocked Hitler's path to power: the venerable father figure Hindenburg, who referred to the Brown Shirt leader as the "Bohemian Corporal"; and the Reichswehr, the elite hundred-thousand-man army that the brilliant martinet, General Hans von Seeckt, had so carefully nurtured. The army maintained that it was nonpolitical, standing apart from the republic and the republic's enemies. Yet under Seeckt's successor, Kurt von Schleicher, it had come to hold a veto power over a chancellor's tenure. It was indeed at Schleicher's instigation that Brüning had become chancellor.

Lacking any mass support, hoping in vain for some turn in the economic tide, Brüning even considered restoring the monarchy as a dike of stability against the National Socialist flood. At this crucial point the Social Democrats and the trade unions were willing to go along. But the stubborn Hindenburg refused to consider such a step unless his "Lord and Master," William II, was recalled. Brüning would have adopted Ebert's old idea of a regency, but the return of the former Kaiser was impossible, and the Hohenzollern moment passed.

In 1932 Hindenburg's seven-year presidential term expired, and though he was now eighty-four, he seemed the only sure alternative to Hitler in the coming election. Reluctantly he agreed to stand again. At this election the monarchist marshal found himself supported by the Social Democrats, the Centrists, and the remnants of the middle-class parties, the very ones that had opposed him seven years earlier. Again the Communists ran Thälmann. It was the bitterest, most savage electoral campaign the country had seen. Yet in spite of the Brown Shirt bully boys, and Goebbels' brilliant propaganda efforts, Hitler received only a third of the vote. Since Hindenburg had failed by a fraction of a per cent to obtain the legally required majority, a run-off election was necessary. This time the president received 53 per cent (19,359,983 votes) to 36.8 for Hitler and 10.2 for Thälmann. The liberal *Berliner Tageblatt* proclaimed the result a "triumph of reason." Encouraged by the results, Brüning a month later suppressed Hitler's Storm Troop army. Reason, it seemed, had triumphed still further.

For a time Hindenburg had considered Brüning the best chancellor since Bismarck, but following the election their relationship cooled. Hindenburg, who had been presented with his family's lapsed estate in East Prussia, cast his lot increasingly with the Junkers, whose bankrupt estates had long been sustained by secret government grants, the so-called East Help, on the grounds that such large-scale farming areas were essential in case of war. Brüning's plan to split up some of these estates and settle unemployed smallholders on them was seen

DER DEUTSCHE STUDENT
KÄMPFT
FÜR FÜHRER UND VOL
N DER MANNSCHAFT DES NSD-STUDENTENBUN

by the Junkers as "agrarian Bolshevism." Their appeal to their landsman, Hindenburg, would precipitate Brüning's curt dismissal two and a half months after Hindenburg's re-election.

A swirl of intrigue now enveloped Hindenburg, the rigid and failing old man being persuaded by his scheming, none-too-bright son Oscar and his all-too-bright presidential secretary Otto Meissner. To succeed Brüning he appointed the debonair, ex-cavalry officer Franz von Papen. Beyond his graceful manners and superficial charms, Papen was a shallow society figure who had demonstrated his professional ineptness as early as 1915 when he was military attaché in the United States. No one had ever taken him seriously, nor did politicians take seriously his "cabinet of barons," nonentities whom he picked, hoping to run Germany as it had been run in the Kaiser's time.

Meanwhile, Hitler conferred variously with Papen, with Schleicher —who emerged from the shadows at last to become minister of defense—and with Hindenburg himself. In exchange for Hitler's passive acquiescence in the Papen ministry, the chancellor lifted the ban on the Storm Troopers and called for still another round of Reichstag elections. That violent campaign saw hundreds injured and about two hundred killed. Again the National Socialists swelled their vote total, becoming the first party in the Reichstag with 230 seats, still 75 short of a majority. Hitler was offered the post of vice-chancellor but continued to demand all or nothing.

Still another election followed in November. This time the National Socialists lost two million votes. With their decline the pace of intrigue quickened. Schleicher himself replaced the inept and unpopular Papen, determined as chancellor to rule directly, with the army behind him and with the president's support. Though devious, Schleicher was an intelligent man, his aims plausible and his intentions of the best. Called by some "the Red General," he initiated talks with trade union leaders, declaring that he supported neither capitalism nor socialism. His aim was a base of support that would include the moderate Socialists, the Catholic Center, the trade unions, and the more reasonable Nazis such as the socialist-minded and soon-to-be-expelled Gregor Strasser. He planned, among other things, a program of public works, a resettlement of some 25,000 peasants on 800,000 bankrupt East Prussian acres. In a broadcast to the nation he asked his listeners not to think of

A recruiting poster for Hitler's National Student Organization urges young men to "fight for Führer and nation."

him as a soldier but as "the impartial trustee of the interests of all in an emergency." He announced that he would be in office for a long time to come. He lasted just fifty-seven days.

Even as Schleicher had undermined Papen, the latter, as Hindenburg's next-door social favorite, was able to reach the old man's ear. It was through Papen's further intrigues, abetted by Oscar von Hindenburg and state secretary Meissner, that the president was finally persuaded on January 30, 1930, to name Hitler chancellor. Only two cabinet posts went to National Socialists. The remaining eight posts went to old-line conservatives, who were counted on to keep Hitler and his lieutenants in line, to give them a sense of governmental responsibility without too much power, and to get rid of them if they failed to cooperate. Papen had let the wild beast out of the cage, to his superficial mind the first step in training the animal.

Hitler, the new chancellor, was then forty-three years old. Twenty years earlier this demonic Austrian-born ranter for racism and German nationalism had been a derelict, lodged in a Vienna doss house, and eking out the thinnest of livings by painting scenic postcards and doing odd jobs of portering. As a boy he had been a failure in school, almost friendless, without talent yet convinced of his destiny as a great artist, a great architect. At a performance of Wagner's *Rienzi* while still at school, he was overwhelmed by the thought of his future destiny as tribune of the people. Lonely, full of envy and hate at the rich world about him, yet contemptuous of the workers, he acquired all the Austrian German's bias against the other races of their polyglot empire. With a quick, shallow mind incapable of sustained intellectual effort, he absorbed the prejudices of the gutter press which he combined with his inner resentments. Imbued with secondhand Darwinism, a smattering of Nietzsche, and the Aryan supremacy notions of Count Gobineau and Houston Stewart Chamberlain, he admired force and intractable leadership, while detesting socialism, democracy, parliamentarianism, the Hapsburg monarchy, and his doss house companions. Above all he hated the Jews, whom he saw as personified devils, the source of all evils of society. In his paranoid dreams, he continued to see himself as the chosen leader destined to mold a greater Germany. Such delusions are not uncommon to drifters and psychopaths, yet his mad dreams he would bring to reality. In that was his sinister genius.

He had left Vienna, and July, 1914, found him in Munich. The outbreak of the war was for him a personal salvation for which he felt ready to get down on his knees in gratitude. At last his meaningless life had a meaning. In the army he found a home and family, food, shelter, clothing, and a sense of unity and belonging. As a soldier he was almost pathologically conscientious though without initiative. A message runner, a lance corporal who was twice wounded, he won the Iron Cross Second Class and later claimed to have won the First Class. Germany's defeat in World War I he was to blame on the Socialists, the Jews, the civilian traitors, and parliamentary backstabbers.

It took the chaos of postwar Bavaria to bring out his latent self. In that time and place of political chaos, he, the fanatic nationalist, discovered that he had the gift of swaying men by his subrational compulsive oratory. Instinctively he pitched on the lowest common denominator of emotional appeals. His party, made up at first of the misfits, the rejects, the adventurers, the soldiers of fortune and misfortune, grew, expanded, developed its symbols, its blood-lust flag with the swirling swastika, its incredible "Heil Hitler!" greeting that intruded his name whenever two followers met. The doss house vagabond now rode in a six-wheeled Mercedes and carried a rhinoceros-hide whip with him as a symbol. Within five years he, the former lance corporal, shared the Beer Hall Putsch with General Ludendorff. In the brief prison sentence that he served after that fiasco, he wrote *Mein Kampf,* that ungrammatical compendium of paranoid ravings, shrewd political observations, and openly stated intentions so bizarre that the world did not take them seriously until it was too late.

Those who had opened the doors of the chancellery to him on that fateful January day hoped to make use of him, confident that they could tame the wild beast. The news of his accession spread like a fire. That evening the pallid man with the Chaplin mustache and the unruly forelock and the wolf's eyes stood in his upper chancellery window, his right arm raised in salute, as seemingly endless ranks of chanting Storm Troopers paraded past him. Carrying torches, marching from the Brandenburg Gate down the Wilhelmstrasse, they moved along like some great luminous serpent. There was a cold look of exultation on Hitler's face as he watched them, a mixture of pride and triumph, fierce elemental joy and vengeful hate.

CHAPTER XIII

FROM WAR TO PEACE

The day after Hindenburg had appointed Hitler chancellor, Ludendorff telegraphed a dark prophecy to his old comrade-in-arms: "I predict in all earnestness that this accursed man will push our empire into the abyss, will cause our nation boundless misery and that coming generations will curse you in your grave for what you have done." Papen and his colleagues had thought they could use Hitler for their anachronistic end of restoring a Wilhelmian Germany. Within weeks they learned otherwise. Vice-Chancellor Papen was also premier of Prussia controlling two thirds of Germany, and he gave little thought to the fact that Hitler's lieutenant, Hermann Göring, the plump vainglorious World War One ace, was Prussian minister of the interior. As such Göring controlled the police, and he used his power ruthlessly to undermine Papen and purge his opponents. Storm Troopers were appointed police auxiliaries and let loose to hunt down their enemies and opponents. Later Göring would organize his own secret police, the dreaded Gestapo, after the Russian model. Since Hitler still lacked a parliamentary majority, he ordered new elections for March 5. It was a campaign in which all the resources of the state, the radio, and

Dürer's "Four Horsemen of the Apocalypse"—Death, Famine, Pestilence, and War—were once again familiar specters with the coming of World War II.

the press were at the disposal of his National Socialists. The Brown Shirts and the even more sinister though fewer black-uniformed SS men (the elite military unit of the party) were given free rein to intimidate the opposition. Violence flared, culminating in the burning of the Reichstag building, an incendiary act devised by Göring as a pretext to smash the Communist Party. The confused old president was prevailed on to issue emergency decrees suspending free speech and a free press. In spite of all the weighted propaganda efforts, the National Socialists in this last free—if impeded—election received only 44 per cent of the votes, although with the Nationalists they managed to have a bare majority of the deputies. It required a two thirds vote of the Reichstag, however, to alter the Constitution. Hitler, by suppressing the Communists altogether and by bearing down relentlessly on the Centrists, finally achieved passage of his Enabling Act of 1933. Only the Social Democrats voted in opposition.

The Enabling Act gave the chancellor the power to draft and to enact laws, to control the budget, and to negotiate treaties with foreign governments without the consent of the Reichstag. Hitler was now in fact dictator, subject neither to parliament nor president nor to the Papen coterie, whom he privately labeled "feudal gamblers and card-sharpers." Only three forces stood between him and absolute unmitigated power: Hindenburg, now obviously tottering to his grave; the Army; and the radical potential of the 4.5 million freebooter Storm Troopers, many times the size of the regular Reichswehr.

Following the Enabling Act, Hitler proceeded to consolidate his rule. Bismarck's federation now became for the first time a single unit, with the states under National Socialist commissioners subordinated to Berlin. All political parties were dissolved except for the National Socialists. Concentration camps expanded across Germany for those opposed to the Third Reich. The Jews were driven from public life, Jewish doctors, lawyers, and teachers being barred from their professions. Free trade unions were replaced by the Labor Front. A People's Court was established in which the protection of the National Socialist regime took precedence over traditional legal concepts.

As for the three counterforces, Hindenburg's would obviously end shortly with his death. Tension grew, however, between the Army and the Storm Troopers, the Army still representing the traditional state while the restive Storm Troopers under their leader Ernst Röhm began to clamor for a second revolution, in which an economic as well as a political upheaval would come about. Röhm wanted his Brown Shirts incorporated into the Reichswehr to make it a people's army, and his troopers wanted the spoils which they felt the January revolution had largely denied them. The climax came, after months of indecision on Hitler's part, in the Blood Purge of June 30, 1934, in which the Führer turned on his followers. Röhm and most of the SA leaders were summarily shot by SS executioners. For three days Germany endured a blood bath in which not only the Brown Shirt leaders but many private and potential enemies were liquidated. Brüning, warned in time, had already escaped to Switzerland. Kurt von Schleicher and his wife were shot down in the doorway of their suburban villa, an indirect warning to the Army. Papen barely managed to escape with his life.

A little over a month later Hindenburg died. Hitler now assumed the office of president as well as chancellor, although he preferred to style himself Führer (leader). On Hindenburg's death all the soldiers and officers of the Reichswehr were commanded to swear an oath of personal allegiance to Hitler. No longer would the Army hold itself apart from the state or impose its veto on politicians. The "cabinet of Barons" faded away as one by one its members resigned or were shunted aside. The Führer now held a more absolute and undisputed power in Germany than had any king or emperor.

Hitler was one of a line of conquerors like Genghis Khan who to the sorrow of mankind appear suddenly in history and build their empires on a pile of skulls. His aim was to prepare Germany for what he welcomed as an inevitable war that would revenge the defeat of 1918. He envisioned a master race of 200 million Aryan Germans who would expand to rule the world. Like a sorcerer or magician, he put Germany under his spell. The majority that he never found in a free election, he soon found in fact. He had promised the Germans work and he gave them work, first through projects much akin to the Work Projects Administration and Public Works Administration of Roosevelt's New Deal, later increasingly through rearmament. Where the republic had not been able to find the money for such projects he conjured it up through his minister of economics, the Nationalist banker Hjalmar Schacht, a financial wizard whose monetary sleight of hand would be accurately defined later by the economist William Röpke as "repressed inflation." Germans had jobs and a renewed feeling of pride in themselves and their country. They were given youth programs, women's programs, a glittering new army, parades, Strength through Joy holidays, new auto roads, and the promise of a people's car—a Volkswagen—for every German workman. They were deafened and bemused by the minister of propaganda, Dr. Goebbels. After the one-year moratorium proposed by President Hoover in 1931, World War I reparations payments had never been resumed and industry hummed as Germany bustled and marched. There was a vague awareness of darker undercurrents; the corrupt life of the leaders; the beatings, the arbitrary arrests and the concentration camps; the noose drawn tighter about the Jews. But these were matters that Every-German preferred not to think about while warming himself in the glow of the Third Reich.

Hitler seemed to move from strength to strength, with the intuitiveness of a gifted politician sensing the weakness of his opponents, and with an adventurer's daring that appalled his generals, making one bold successful stroke after another. Quietly he began to rearm. In October, 1933, Germany withdrew from the Geneva Disarmament Conference, begun the year before Hitler came to power, and followed this by quitting the League of Nations. Seventeen months later Hitler denounced the disarmament clauses of the Treaty of Versailles and announced the expansion of the armed forces and the reintroduction of conscription. The League of Nations condemned this action, but nothing else happened. With France distracted by social strife, the British in a mood of pacifism and appeasement, the United States preoccupied with the Depression, and Russia in the grip of the Great Purge, there was no tangible opposition to the growing German might. In January, 1935, in a plebiscite conducted by the League of Nations, over 90 per cent of the Saarlanders voted for reunion with Germany. Fourteen months later Hitler audaciously, over the protests of his generals, sent his troops into the demilitarized Rhineland. The German Army was not yet strong enough to resist a French attack, but Hitler gambled on the irresolution of the French leaders.

In the furor that followed, it seemed briefly that France might invade the Rhineland—as a preventive measure—but in the end the vacillating French government, lacking support from the British, did nothing more than protest. Hitler, having taken his measure of the democracies, astutely prepared his next move. He arranged an Anti-Comintern Pact with Italy and Japan. In February, 1938, in a bloodless purge of his generals, he removed the more independent-minded staff officers and himself assumed direct command of the armed forces. One month later he sent his army across the Austrian border "to restore my dear homeland to the German Reich." The Austrians did not resist the *Anschluss,* and French and British protests were muted. The Greater Germany, the dream of the War of Liberation and of 1848, had become a cruel reality under the swastika.

Next the Führer turned his attentions to Czechoslovakia, where more than three million Germans lived within the western and northern Czech borders. These Sudeten Germans, at Hitler's urging, now began a systematic and violent agitation against the central government at Prague. But Czechoslovakia was a much harder nut to crack than Austria. The country was well armed, well fortified behind its mountain barriers, and internationally secured by a military alliance with France. In addition the Czechs had an agreement with Russia for military assistance contingent on French aid. The Sudeten Germans had first demanded autonomy. Now they demanded reunion with Germany. Clashes between the Sudeten Germans and the Czech police became miniature battles. Hitler threatened war. France's premier Édouard Daladier warned that if Czechoslovakia was attacked the French would fight. In May there were rumors of German troop movements, and the Czech government ordered a partial mobilization.

England's prime minister, the Birmingham businessman Neville Chamberlain, felt that England must back up France, but he also thought that Czechoslovakia was not worth a war, and he pressed the unwilling Czech government to make concessions. He believed that the Sudetenland should be given to Germany, even though the loss of that mountainous region would leave Czechoslovakia indefensible. The spring crisis passed but Hitler's war of nerves continued as the rivalry in the Sudetenland rose to the pitch of insurrection. The feeling grew that the German dictator would send his troops over the Czech border in September. His speeches grew more ominous. Twice Chamberlain flew to see him in the hopes of preserving peace. Hitler repeat-

edly demanded the annexation of the Sudetenland, and each time he upped his demands. With Czechoslovakia's order of full mobilization, Europe seemed teetering on the brink of war. At the last minute Hitler agreed to meet with Chamberlain and Daladier at a conference in Munich. There on the twenty-ninth of September, with Mussolini also present, Chamberlain and Daladier yielded to the substance of Hitler's demands. The Czechs were to surrender all areas where more than half the inhabitants were Germans, such areas to be designated by Hitler. The new frontiers would be guaranteed by France, England, Germany, and Italy. By the settlement Germany gained some 3,500,000 Sudetens, of whom 700,000 were Czechs, and the lion's share of Czech industry. More important, Hitler was able to seize the intricate network of border fortifications without which Czechoslovakia was no more than a defenseless rump state, a German satellite. To Chamberlain and Daladier, as well as to most Englishmen and Frenchmen at the time, the all-important thing was that war had been avoided. "I have no more territorial demands on Europe," Hitler informed Chamberlain.

Hitler arrives at a Nazi Party rally in September, 1934. Crowd psychology and impressive sound and sight demonstrations almost hypnotize followers.

"Peace in our time," Chamberlain told a cheering crowd as he held up the signed pact on his return to England. The somber, elderly prime minister in the wing collar and clutching a tightly furled umbrella would become a symbol of appeasement. In his moment of return his countrymen believed him. But there was little indication of peace in the renewed violence of Hitler's speeches nor in the November Night of Broken Glass, the worst yet of the German pogroms, in which Jewish shop windows were smashed, the synagogues destroyed, and Jews by the thousands tortured and dragged off to concentration camps. Five and a half months after the "peace in our time," Hitler, on pretense of keeping order, sent his troops into Prague and proclaimed a German protectorate over the truncated country. Czechoslovakia was swallowed up. Poland, it now became clear, was his next goal.

Chamberlain, bitter over Czechoslovakia's fate, announced that the German action was a complete repudiation of the Munich agreement. In fear of further expansion by an increasingly powerful Germany that would one day turn westward, the prime minister signed an agreement with Poland that would give that country the automatic support of England and France if Germany should attack. In the months of fumbling diplomacy that followed, France and England sought an alliance with the Soviet Union to contain Germany. Stalin refused to commit himself or his country. Meanwhile, secret negotiations were going on between the ostensible archenemies, the Germans and the Russians. Undoubtedly Stalin hoped for a mutually exhausting war between Germany and the West, after which he would be left to pick up the pieces. But beyond that, the brown dictator and the red dictator, for all their mutual vilification, privately admired one another. Their ways were similar. They were both amoral adventurers who had used a revolutionary impulse to climb to power. In that summer of 1939 they were ready to divide Europe between them.

The German-Soviet nonaggression and trade pact of August 23, 1939, was the most startling coup in a century of European diplomacy, a reversal as sudden as if black had suddenly become white. Yet from a long perspective it was not outside the German tradition, for in the 1922 Treaty of Rapallo the two then-outcast nations had come together, and during the twenties the Reichswehr had secretly conducted intensive training inside Russia with weapons forbidden by Versailles. But, for the "Boss" of world Communism and the Führer of Anti-Bolshevism to form an alliance of friendship left the French and British in helpless astonishment. So quick was the transformation in Moscow that swastika banners had to be borrowed from an anti-Nazi play then running (and immediately suppressed) in order to deck the airport for the arrival of Joachim von Ribbentrop, the ex-champagne salesman who had become Hitler's foreign minister. At a Kremlin reception after the pact was signed, Stalin amiably raised his glass to Ribbentrop, saying: "I know how much the German nation loves its Führer. I should therefore like to drink to his health." Stalin's foreign minister, Vyacheslav Molotov, remarked that it was "a matter of taste whether a worker is Communist or National Socialist."

Hitler's pact with Russia freed him from the fear that had haunted Bismarck, that had shadowed Berlin in the summer of 1914—a war on two fronts. In the weeks preceding completion of this accord, the Führer drew up plans for the speedy conquest and annihilation of Poland. In a secret subpact the two dictators had divided the country and the spoils. Poland would go Czechoslovakia's way of oblivion, the Baltic states and Rumanian Bessarabia would fall to Russia. Stalin as part of the deal would deliver oil and raw materials to Germany. Hitler, still hoping to persuade the British and the French to stay out of the war, still pretending to a reasonableness, postponed the invasion of Poland from the last week in August to September 1. His demands on Poland, including Danzig, the Corridor, and Silesia, he knew the Poles would not accept. While his Army mobilized, the German press was full of accounts of Polish atrocities. Early on the morning of September 1, 1939, the German Army crossed the Polish border. France and England made ready to declare war. In London Chamberlain, his dreams of peace in ruins, notified Berlin that unless the German forces withdrew, a state of war would exist between Great Britain and Germany. On Sunday, September 3, he spoke over the air to the nation, his flat and infinitely weary voice announcing that no reply had been received from Berlin and that consequently "I have to tell you that . . . this country is at war with Germany."

The mood of August, 1914, had been one of joy, release, with crowds surging through the streets cheering and singing. In September, 1939, the streets of London, Paris, and Berlin were silent, empty.

Men still young enough to fight had fought in that other war, women still young were old enough to remember, and the feeling now was not of fulfillment but of apprehension and doom. Admiral Wilhelm Canaris, the anti-Nazi head of German military intelligence, confided to an acquaintance that "this means the end of Germany."

The war's opening was a Hitler fantasy come true. While the French Army remained quiescent behind its Maginot Line, the German Army overran Poland in less than four weeks. For all the quixotic bravery of the Poles, their cavalry and old-style infantry regiments could offer no ordered resistance to a blitzkrieg of mechanized divisions and dive bombers. Following the first German sweep, the Russians invaded from the east to meet the Germans at a prearranged line. German losses in the campaign were small. Poland was once again partitioned.

That winter, marked only by the Russian attack on Finland, was the deceptively quiet period known as the Phony War. The French faced Germany's hastily constructed West Wall with wary passivity. In England rearmament speeded up, but ordinary life went on much the same. There were those who thought the war might well end in an armed stalemate. Then in April, with cold suddenness, German sea and air forces invaded Norway while the army at the same time occupied Denmark. Within weeks Norwegian resistance was broken. That campaign was only a prelude to the May assault, when German armies without warning smashed through Holland, Belgium, and Luxemburg, flanking the Maginot Line, driving a British Expeditionary Force into the Dunkirk perimeter and cutting deep into France. Though German forces were actually inferior numerically both in men and tanks, the French generals were still fighting the 1914–18 war and were unable to counter Hitler's blitz tactics of ranging tanks and mechanical infantry. In five weeks the campaign was over and the French had capitulated, Hitler forcing them to sign the surrender in the very railway car where the Germans had signed the armistice after World War I.

The Führer returned to Berlin in triumph. Children scattered rose-petals before his six-wheeled Mercedes as he drove down Unter den Linden. All the doubts and hesitancies of the previous September were forgotten in this tremendous victory. With fewer casualties even than Germany had sustained in the Franco-Prussian War, he had reversed the verdict of 1918. The German Army appeared invincible, and

Germany the master of Europe. Immediately after the fall of France at least 90 per cent of the German people were behind Hitler, "the greatest commander of all times." So he saw himself. The atheist, the gutter-Caesar, believed in what he called providence, his destiny as a world conqueror. Germany was merely the instrument of his will. He had overriden the professional caution of his generals so many times that he now considered himself a military genius as well as a man of destiny. He had translated the paranoid dreamings of a Vienna tramp to a brutal and encompassing reality. Genius he did have; the mesmeric personality, and the instinct for the weakness of his opponents. But what he thought of as destiny and providence was far more luck. It was Hitler's luck that the French did not move when he reoccupied the Rhineland, that Chamberlain had flown to Munich even as a group of anti-Nazi generals were preparing to depose him, that the France of 1940 was rotten from within. Yet, imperceptibly, his luck had already turned by the autumn of 1940. He had expected after the fall of France to come to terms with a defeated England, making what he considered a generous offer as he admired the British. But alone and against all odds, though indirectly supported by the United States, the British refused to consider themselves defeated. Instead they shunted Chamberlain aside and made Winston Churchill prime minister.

Hitler's 1940 air attacks against England failed, though the Luftwaffe in more competent hands than those of the pompous Göring might have succeeded in winning the Battle of Britain. If so, according to Air Marshall Hugh Dowding, Germany would have won the war. At that, it was a close call, a matter of a few hundred R.A.F. fighter pilots who outflew and outfought their German rivals and saved the day. Faced with this contretemps, Hitler postponed a decision in the West to renew his old dream of Lebensraum in the East. On June 22, 1941, the German Army marched over the 2,000-mile-long Russian border. That army was the greatest military machine the world had ever seen, in the last great classical campaign.

Military experts predicted Russia would be defeated in six weeks. Hitler, expecting victory before the leaves fell, made no provision for winter clothing or equipment. At first the German advance seemed a repetition of the 1940 blitz. The Wehrmacht took Smolensk, and the road to Moscow lay open. Russian armies were annihilated, hundreds of thousands of prisoners taken. If Hitler had left his generals to their own devices, they would have taken Moscow and no doubt have established a line to mitigate the worst rigors of the Russian winter. But as supreme commander he scattered his objectives. He wanted Leningrad, Moscow, and the Ukraine all at once. His Russian intelligence reports were faulty, his supplies and reinforcements inadequate for anything but a blitzkrieg. The brilliance of the initial advance was deceptive.

As the first German troops thrust into the Ukraine they were hailed as liberators and offered the traditional bread and salt as they passed. If Hitler had been prudent enough to treat his prisoners and the masses of disaffected Russians with consideration, he could have won loyal allies that might have made the overthrow of Stalin possible. Instead, with his racial mania, he persisted in regarding the Russians as "Slav vermin" and Untermenschen (subhumans), fit only to exist as serfs if at all. Behind the Wehrmacht came the terrible SS Einsatz squads, the executioners, liquidators of Jews and Slavs. By his manic brutality Hitler united the Russians against him, impelling them into growing ranks of anti-Nazi partisans.

The Führer, relying on his intuition, had spread himself too thin, with divisions policing occupied Europe, an army in North Africa, and Britain an increasing threat. His act of folly in declaring war on the United States in December, 1941, sealed his fate, although this fate was not apparent until the end of his 1942 Russian campaign that started out with sweeping territorial advances and finished with the loss of an army at Stalingrad. Stalingrad had been preceded by the defeat of his Afrika Corps at El Alamein. After this twin loss there could no longer be any hope of victory, as many Germans now darkly sensed. In the following spring the Russians moved over to a counter-offensive. The next two years saw the inevitable tightening of the noose, the steady advance of the Russians toward and finally into Germany, the capitulation of the Afrika Corps, the D-Day landings of the British and Americans, followed by the liberation of France and Belgium and the south of Holland. And while the Allies closed in, their bombers rained destruction on the German cities.

As Germany slid toward ruin and defeat, the Führer grew more and more out of touch with reality, his paranoid fancies in the end bearing as little relation to fact as had his doss house dreams in prewar Vienna.

After Count Klaus von Stauffenberg, one of a group of anti-Nazi conspirators and dissident army officers, had placed a bomb in Hitler's headquarters on July 20, 1944, Hitler attributed his lucky survival to "providence." Almost to the end he refused to face the fact of defeat, continually looking to some sudden stroke of fortune to save him. When the Russians late in April, 1945, finally closed in on his bunker in Berlin, he knew that the end had indeed come and he shot himself. Eva Braun, his mistress of years and wife of a few hours, died with him. His last wish had been to destroy Germany with himself in a vast Wagnerian holocaust. The Third Reich, that he boasted would last a thousand years, had lasted just twelve.

With Hitler's death the sorcerer's spell was broken. Suddenly the Third Reich appeared as incredible as it had been monstrous. For all those vast crowds that had once hailed their Führer with virtual hysteria, it was now almost impossible to find a National Socialist in Germany. What was left was a desolation unequalled since the end of the Thirty Years' War. The great cities resembled extinct craters. From east and west the invading armies moved in. A week after Hitler's suicide German army leaders surrendered according to Roosevelt's demand for Unconditional Surrender and the German government ceased to exist. "We come as conquerors," said General Eisenhower. The victors brought a Carthaginian peace that seemed the more justified as the details of the concentration camps and the gas chambers and the extermination of millions were brought to light. Germans were pariahs, not even to be spoken to except in the way of official business. So they were treated by the Western forces. From the East vengeful, undisciplined Russian soldiers marched into Germany, plundering raping, and destroying as they went—the Germans were fair game.

With the occupation an Allied Control Council of British, American, Russian, and French commanders filled the vacuum of authority. With Poland having seized East Prussia, Silesia, and parts of Pomerania and Brandenburg, and Russia having annexed the northern part of East Prussia including Königsberg, what remained was a truncated Germany. It was divided into four zones, Russia holding the region east of the Elbe, Great Britain the northwest and the industrial Ruhr, the United States Hesse and most of southern Germany and France, the narrow sections of Württemberg, Baden, and the Rhineland. Ber-

A Russian soldier waves the Hammer and Sickle atop the Reichstag as a shattered Berlin surrenders to the Soviets on May 2, 1945.

lin, located deep within the Russian zone, was also split in four.

In July Stalin met at Potsdam with the new leaders of England and the United States, Prime Minister Clement Attlee and President Harry Truman, to attempt to establish a common policy for Germany in regard to disarmament, demilitarization, reparations, and the renewal of democratic political life. The attempt was doomed, as the erstwhile allies would soon discover, for what Stalin understood by "democratic" was a Bolshevized Germany, a people's republic subservient to Moscow. In the wake of Potsdam, ten to twelve million Germans were expelled from their homes in Poland, Czechoslovakia, and Hungary. These empty-handed "expellees" thrust across the border into a starving country were planned by Stalin as a further means of reducing Germany to a desperation that would be succeeded by Communism. Two years of hunger followed the Potsdam Conference, years in which hordes of homeless, tattered people crisscrossed the ruined landscape, riding in trains little better than cattle cars, sleeping in fouled air raid shelters, finding no end to their journeyings. Supposedly the daily food ration was 1,500 calories. Rarely did it reach that. Money was worthless, the cigarette becoming the one standard of value. The policy of "denazification" with its endless questionnaires seemed a cruel joke.

During those years, at a local and then a *Land* or state level, the political parties were reconstituted first in the Russian zone and two months later in the Western zones. Four major parties representing the left and center reappeared. The Catholic Center reappeared as the more encompassing middle-class Christian Democratic Union. A small party, the Free Democrats, continued vaguely in the tradition of Stresemann's National Liberals. The Social Democrats and the Communists represented the more radical interests. Some of the older German *Länder* were revived, the smaller ones consolidated, new ones created—a total of eleven in the Western zones, five in the Eastern zone—and in 1947 the Allied Control Council formally dissolved Prussia, the very symbol of militant Germany. In that same year the British and Americans combined their zones, to which the French zone was later added. By March, 1948, relations with the Soviet Union had so deteriorated that the Russians withdrew from the Control Council and blockaded road access to Berlin. Against all Stalin's expectations the Allies were able to supply the city by an airlift, flying in cargoes night and day for over a year in a shuttle system that finally compelled the Russians to give up the blockade. From enemies, the Berliners in their defiance of the U.S.S.R. during the airlift had become heroes in the eyes of many Westerners. But by the end of the lift the two Germanys were well established: monolithic East Germany, where the Social Democrats had been forced to join the Communists in the Socialist Unity Party, with all other parties to be suppressed; and the nascent Western Federal Republic.

The turning point for Western Germany came in the summer of 1948 when a new and solid currency—the Deutsche Mark—was introduced at a rate of 10 to 100 for the old Reichsmark of the Hitler era. Overnight, ordinary things again had value. Goods came out of hiding. The currency reform, aided by a massive infusion of Marshall Aid funds, released the German qualities of order, diligence, and enterprise. Professor Ludwig Erhard, the economic director of the combined English-American zone, proceeded to eliminate the whole ingrown system of financial and economic controls then in operation, much to the dismay of London and Washington planners who had visualized a socialized welfare state on the English model. But Erhard's bold stroke liberated energies that in a dozen years would make Western Germany the leading industrial nation of Europe and the third industrial power in the world. Although in 1948 the average German might still be poor and ill-sheltered, at least he could eat and buy something for his wages. For this he was overwhelmingly grateful. After the atrocious years, workers' demands were both modest and restrained, and Germany in returning to a market economy and market discipline was able to avoid the all-too-familiar Western pattern of the wage-price spiral.

In 1948 sixty-five "founding fathers," representatives of the eleven lands, met at Bonn to draft the Basic Law of the new democratic Federal Republic. The small and sleepy Rhineland city, Beethoven's birthplace, was chosen as a provisional capital that would be shifted to Berlin once Western and Eastern Germany were reunited in a Fourth Reich. After the Basic Law had been adopted, elections followed. Under the new bicameral system, seats in the popularly elected lower house—the Bundestag—and an indirectly elected upper house representing the states—the Bundesrat—were filled. The initial election brought the Christian Democrats a small lead over the Social Democrats and gave them the first chancellor of the Federal Republic, the 73-year-old Konrad Adenauer whose career dated back to Kaiser William's day. He had been elected a member of the Cologne city council in 1906, and had served as lord mayor from 1917 to 1933, when he was removed from office by the National Socialists. In retirement he never concealed his contempt for Hitler, and toward the end of the war spent some months in a concentration camp. With the reconstitution of the political parties, the Catholic and Conservative Adenauer emerged as leader of the Christian Democratic Union. An austere, patriarchal figure, honored rather than loved, a patriot rather than a nationalist, Adenauer strove to restore his country to prosperity and respectability. Working to regain German sovereignty, achieved with the departure of the last high commissioner in 1955 (who had in turn replaced the Allied military governors), he saw that sovereignty as a prelude to German participation in a United States of Europe. In spite of his country's general reluctance to rearm, he created with U.S. urging the democratic-oriented Bundeswehr. He brought West Germany into the North Atlantic Treaty Organization and the European Coal and Steel Community. In 1963 he signed a Reconciliation Treaty with France. He undertook retribution payments to Israel for the monstrous acts of the Hitler era. For fourteen years "Der Alte," the Old Man, with the assistance of his economic minister Ludwig Erhard, guided the Federal Republic to the abundance of the "economic miracle." An adroit, even at times a slippery, politician, Adenauer, with his party slogan of "Prosperity for everyone," stultified the opposition. Not only was the booming industrialism of the truncated Federal Republic able to absorb the millions of refugees but it even found it necessary to import several million foreigners to fill the growing shortage of workers.

For Adenauer in Bonn the shadow of the larger Reich still lurked behind the sunny prosperity of the smaller republic. The other Germany, the German Democratic Republic that had been founded under Russian auspices, he treated as nonexistent and refused to consider Germany's eastern boundaries as other than they had been in 1937. In contrast to the prosperity of the West, East Germany, a Russian satellite, bound by dogma to collectivism and state ownership, and denuded by Russian requisitions, had made only halting progress toward recovery. On June 16, 1953, the workers of East Berlin revolted against increased work norms, burned pictures of their hated chief of state Walter Ulbricht, and tore down the red flag from the Brandenburg Gate. The revolt spread to Halle, Magdeburg, Dresden. When Russian tanks moved against the East Germans, they replied with cobblestones. Foredoomed to failure the revolt has been memorialized in the West as a Day of National Unity. East Germans were at least able to vote with their feet, and even when they could no longer slip over the mined zonal borders, it was still possible to take the subway from East Berlin to West Berlin. By 1961 some 3,500,000 workers, technicians, doctors, farmers, engineers, and intellectuals—the more educated and younger groups in the German Democratic Republic—had made their way from East to West. Then, in August of that year, the East German police and units of the East German People's Army closed the subway and sealed off their section of the city with the Berlin Wall, that concrete barrier that has become the symbol of Communist oppression. Once the escape hatch was closed, those who remained were thrown back on themselves, to make the best of what they had even though they hated it.

During the Adenauer years the Social Democrats seemed on the way to remaining the permanent opposition that they were under the monarchy. Material prosperity confounded the Marxist dogma of the growing misery of the proletariat. German workers, once among the most politically minded in Europe, were increasingly apolitical. The people's car of glib Nazi promises had become a reality for most families. Men preferred Sunday afternoon drives to political meetings.

After a severe election setback in 1957, the younger Social Democratic leaders decided that even the party's watered-down version of Marxism and socialism was not enough. In 1959 at a party convention at Bad Godesberg the old dogmas were unceremoniously junked. No longer was there talk of a nationalization of key industries and of a planned economy. The Social Democrats now declared that "free competition and free enterprise are important elements of economic policy." Gone from the convention were the red flags and banners, gone even the proletarian greeting of "Comrade." The goal of the Social Democratic Party now was to attract dissident middle-class votes.

After Adenauer's retirement in 1963, Ludwig Erhard became chancellor in a coalition government with the Free German Party. But

Erhard, the skillful economics minister, proved himself singularly inept as chancellor, and three years later the Free Germans left the coalition, bringing about his downfall. Meanwhile the slowly growing popularity of the Social Democrats had been demonstrating the wisdom of their Bad Godesberg policy. New and dynamic leaders were replacing the older routine party officials. Most dynamic among them was Willy Brandt, the former mayor of West Berlin. An astute, undogmatic man of great personal charm, he was able to form a link between two generations. Illegitimate, born in 1913 under another name, as an adolescent he became a Social Democratic militant, later a reporter for a Socialist paper, and when Hitler came to power he fled to Norway and then Sweden. Returning after the war as a German correspondent for the Scandinavian press, he resumed his German citizenship, re-entered politics, and in 1957 was elected mayor of Berlin. Erhard's downfall was Brandt's opportunity, for the two major parties, rivals rather than adversaries, pragmatically buried their differences to form a Grand Coalition, with the Christian Socialist civil servant Kurt Georg Kiesinger as chancellor and Brandt as vice-chancellor and foreign minister. The economic policy of the coalition insured the country's continued prosperity by judicious pump priming while at the same time balancing the budget. A start was made on overdue penal, judicial, and educational reforms. But the real new direction was in the field of foreign affairs. After Stalin's death, Adenauer had gone to Moscow and established diplomatic relations with the Soviet Union. Nevertheless, under what was known as the Hallstein Doctrine, he insisted that any state subsequently recognizing the German Democratic Republic would cease to be recognized diplomatically by the West German government. When in 1957 Yugoslavia recognized Eastern Germany, Adenauer at once severed relations. Foreign Minister Brandt discarded this rigid cold-war attitude, moving to "change through rapprochements" with the East-bloc nations, recognizing Rumania and again exchanging envoys with Yugoslavia.

In the Bundestag elections of 1969 the Social Democrats received a disappointing 42.7 per cent of the vote to 46.1 per cent for the Christian Democrats. Then, against all expectations, the Free Democrats—who had become increasingly restive in their cooperative relations with the Christian Democratic Union—threw their support to the Social

One remaining barrier to peaceful coexistence: the Berlin Wall

Democrats. By a knife-edge coalition majority, the Social Democrats were at last able to assume power for the first time in the history of the 21-year-old Federal Republic. Their leader, Willy Brandt, became chancellor even as he had just about given up hope of ever attaining that office. What Foreign Minister Brandt had indicated as an opening to the East, he now as chancellor made his primary aim. In March, 1970, he attempted to bridge the gap between the two Germanys by visiting East German premier Willi Stoph at Erfurt in East Germany. During the latter part of the year he signed nonaggression treaties with Russia and Poland. Although there had been no diplomatic ties between West Germany and Poland, the Warsaw Treaty went far beyond the political limits of its Moscow counterpart. Its central point was the recognition of the permanence of the Oder-Niesse Line, Poland's western boundary. By this yielding to cold facts Brandt conceded that there was no hope short of war of restoring Germany's 1937 boundaries or of reuniting Germany in a Fourth Reich.

In May, 1972, after months-long and often thorny deliberations between East and West German negotiators, the two states finally agreed on a treaty assuring unimpeded traffic to and from Berlin with the possibility of opening up "broader contractual agreements." A week later the Bundestag ratified the Moscow and Warsaw Treaties, even as the foreign ministers of the United States, the Soviet Union, France, and Britain signed a pact aimed at ending East-West tension over divided Berlin. Earlier there seemed a possibility that Brandt's treaties might be defeated, but the opposition delegates were aware that the chancellor's new Eastern policy had won wide acceptance, and in the actual voting most of the Christian Democrats merely abstained. "Before us is the task that is the central point of our policy," said Chancellor Brandt after the ratification, "attaining improvements in the life of the people of divided Germany, peace at the borders, a normalization of relations between East and West in Germany and Europe."

As Europe moved into the seventies, what had for so long been unthinkable for Germans now became accepted. Germany was now and would remain two nations. The empire, the Reich, was dead. And with that stubborn fact came the increasing awareness that the two Germanys were drifting apart, culturally as well as economically, educationally, even in language where two sets of vocabularies were developing. East Germany with its seventeen million inhabitants was still a police state sealed in by a million and a half border mines and fifty thousand miles of barbed wire. But behind those formidable barriers, it had managed to become the most prosperous nation of the Communist bloc, Europe's sixth power, and the world's seventh. Its younger generation, which would form the future professional and managerial and administrative elite, might be disaffected and scornful of the stale Marxist dogmas taught in school, yet these same young people had no great love or admiration for the other Germany. Freedom indeed they wanted, but not on the Western model.

The Federal Republic, with its sixty million inhabitants, was again the most powerful nation of Western Europe. But the old jack-boot nationalism had gone for good. Once the Army's officer corps had been Germany's most admired caste. Today the Bundeswehr advertises in the newspapers in a vain attempt to meet its quota of officer candidates. To the young of West Germany, Hitler is an incomprehensible adventurer, patriotism itself something that verges on the quaint. As in the rest of Europe the young are disaffected, though in the Federal Republic more on the American model in everything from clothes and haircuts to music and romantic-radical leftist movements.

The prosperity of Western Germany, however pervasive, seems as rootless as the towering buildings of glass and steel that spring out of the ground of the old cities. There are shadows that threaten to take some of the glitter from the economic miracle. In spite of the solid international standing of the mark, creeping inflation moves just a little faster each year. Workers are more restive. Employment dips ever so slightly, but it dips. There are the familiar ecological problems, intensified within the Federal Republic's truncated limits.

Western Germany, in the old geopolitical phrase, remains the heartland of Europe. As the German lands once merged to form an empire, so it seems that the future of this Germany will be to merge into the Europe of Adenauer's vision and Brandt's hope while still retaining its German identity. East Germany now belongs to the East. But doubtless one day, even as Austria and Germany split from the Holy Roman Empire to become in the end kindred neighbors, so will the two fragments of imperial Germany, the Federal and the Democratic Republics, live side by side as sister nations.

CHRONOLOGY

c. 1000–100 B.C.	Germanic and Celtic tribes settle in north and central Europe
c. 55	Julius Caesar makes first important contact with Germanic tribes along the northern frontier of Roman Empire
A.D. 9	Arminius, chief of the Cherusci, defeats Roman legions in Teutoberg Forest; Rome abandons German expansion policy
481–511	Reign of Clovis, king of the Franks; establishes Frankish monarchy, including Gaul and western Germany
672–754	Boniface, archbishop and missionary, spreads Christianity among Germans; organizes eastern Frankish church
800	Charlemagne (Karl der Grosse), resurrector of the Roman Empire of the West, is crowned in Rome by the pope
c. 840	Vikings begin to ravage Europe; their attacks speed up disintegration of the already crumbling Frankish Empire
843	Treaty of Verdun repartitions Frankish Carolingian Empire into three kingdoms; Louis the German receives eastern regions roughly equal to the area of the future German state
919	Henry the Fowler, a Saxon duke, repulses Magyar hordes and is rewarded with the title King of the Germans, inaugurating 105 years of Saxon rule
936–973	Otto I succeeds his father; defeats Magyars at Lechfeld
962	Pope crowns Otto I, emperor of the West, in Rome, establishing precedent for German kings' claim to title of Holy Roman Emperor; start of German involvement in Italian politics
1152–1190	Frederick Barbarossa inaugurates rule of Hohenstaufens, leads army on Third Crusade
1241	Hanseatic League of northern German towns organized
1273	Long struggle over imperial succession ends with Rudolf I, first Hapsburg emperor
1300s	Time of prosperity for German peasants and traders; Hanseatic League now includes ports from Amsterdam to Reval
1356	Charles IV promulgates Golden Bull which remains constitution of Holy Roman Empire until its dissolution in 1806
1415	Emperor Sigismund grants Frederick of Hohenzollern possession of March of Brandenburg and titles Margrave and Elector
fl. 1500	Painters Grünewald, Dürer, Cranach, Holbein
1517	Reformation begins; Martin Luther nails his 95 theses condemning misuse of papal indulgences on Wittenberg church
1521	Diet of Worms orders Luther's arrest; he escapes and translates Bible into German, setting the standard for the modern German language
1555	Peace of Augsburg allows each prince to determine the religion of his own state; temporary cessation of religious wars

1618–1648	Thirty Years' War ends in Peace of Westphalia, which restricts imperial power and remaps much of Europe; Austria and Germany emerge as separate entities
1685–1750	Johann Sebastian Bach
1700	Frederick III of Brandenburg assumes title King of Prussia
1713–1740	Reign of Frederick William I of Prussia, who organizes army
1740–1786	Reign of Frederick the Great; continues father's work in strengthening Prussian state; core of modern Germany forged
1740–1748	War of Austrian Succession; Prussia clashes with Austria
c. 1780	Goethe and Schiller inaugurate the Romantic era in literature
1800	Beethoven composes the first of his nine symphonies
1803–1815	German states drawn into Napoleonic Wars; Prussia crushed by France; Holy Roman Empire is formally dissolved
1810	Friedrich Krupp, ironmaster, founds Krupp Works at Essen
1815	Congress of Vienna; Prussia awarded additional lands including industrial Rhineland; loose confederation of 39 German states replaces welter of 200-odd administrative entities
fl. 1845	Composers Mendelssohn, Schumann, Wagner, Brahms
1848	German states swept by revolution
1862	Otto von Bismarck becomes minister-president of Prussia; he forms Prussian-dominated North German Confederation
1870–1871	Franco-Prussian War; Bismarck defeats France, achieves a united Germany under Prussian leadership; Alsace-Lorraine acquired by Germany
1871	William I of Prussia is declared emperor, or Kaiser, of Germany
1888–1918	Reign of Kaiser William II; Wilhelmian era of prosperity
1914–1919	Germany loses to Allies in World War; Kaiser abdicates
1919	Alsace-Lorraine is returned to France by Treaty of Versailles
1919–1934	Drafting of new constitution and formation of Weimar Republic
1923	Hitler and others launch abortive Beer Hall Putsch in Munich
1929	World economic crisis; depression in Germany
1933	Hitler is appointed chancellor; Third Reich is formed; Reichstag is burned; anti-Semitism becomes official policy
1936	Hitler remilitarizes Rhineland; Rome-Berlin Axis is formed
1938	Hitler annexes Austria and takes Sudetenland from Czechoslovakia
1939	Germany invades Poland; World War II begins
1945	Global war ends in total defeat for Germany; Hitler commits suicide; Allies divide Germany into four occupation zones.
1948	Soviets impose Berlin blockade and U.S. responds with airlift
1949	Federal Republic (West Germany) and Democratic Republic (East Germany) are established
1961	Berlin Wall is built to halt exit of East Germans to the West
1972	East and West Germany sign treaty recognizing each other's sovereignty, redefining borders, and opening the way to enlarged trade and cultural exchanges

CREDITS AND INDEX

2 Base map drawn by Richard Edes Harrison, courtesy of Ginn and Company, a Xerox Company, Lexington, Mass. 4 Coin—Staatliche Münzsammlung, Munich; orb—Kunsthistorisches, Museum, Vienna 5 Statue—The Metropolitan Museum of Art, Gift of Alistair B. Martin, 1948; mount—Trustees of the British Museum 6 The Fogg Museum of Art, Cambridge 13 Bildarchiv Foto Marburg 17 Bibliothèque Nationale 20 Trustees of the British Museum 24–25 Stiftsbibliotek, St-Gall 29 Bibliothèque Nationale, Service Photographique 32 Louvre 36 Metropolitan Museum of Art, Fletcher Fund, 1919 43 Demschatz, Aachen 49 Bibliothèque Nationale 52 Albertina, Vienna 57 Universitatsbibliotek, Heidelberg 62–63 Staatsbibliotek, Munich 68 Speyer Cathedral 74 Kupferstichkabinett, Staatliche Museum, Berlin 81 Lala Aufsberg 86 Universitatsbibliotek, Heidelberg 94 Scala 98 National Gallery of Art, Washington 103 Staatsarchiv, Rathus, Hamburg 106 Schmolz-Huth 111 Vatican Library 114 Albertina, Vienna 119 Stadt Augsburg, Kunstsammlunger 123 Bildarchiv Foto Marburg 126 Trustees of the British Museum 131 Larry Burrows, Life © 1956 Time Inc. 138 Albertina, Vienna 146 Kunsthistorisches Museum, Vienna 150 The Metropolitan Museum of Art, Fletcher Fund, 1919 154–55 Stadtarchiv, Bonn 158 Nymphenburg Palace, Munich 164 The Fogg Museum of Art, Cambridge 169 Krupp—Hachette 177 Thomas Hollyman, Photo Researchers 180 Kunsthalle, Bremen 184 The Museum of Modern Art, Gift of Abby Aldrich Rockefeller 192 Library of Congress 196 The Fogg Museum of Art, Cambridge 202 Library of Congress 208 Sovfoto 214 Leonard Freed—Magnum

Page numbers in **boldface type** refer to illustrations.
Page references to map entries are in *italic type.*